The Small Business Controller

The Small Business Controller

Richard O. Hanson, DBA, CPA, CFE, CMA, CFM

The Small Business Controller

First published in 2009 by
Business Expert Press, LLC
222 East 46th Street, New York, NY 10017
www.businessexpertpress.com

ISBN-13: 978-1-60649-062-4 (paperback)
ISBN-10: 1-60649-062-1 (paperback)

ISBN-13: 978-1-60649-063-1 (e-book)
ISBN-10: 1-60649-063-X (e-book)

DOI 10.4128/9781606490631

A publication in the Business Expert Press Managerial Accounting collection

Collection ISSN (print) forthcoming
Collection ISSN (electronic) forthcoming

Cover design by Artistic Group—Monroe, NY
Interior design by Scribe, Inc.

First edition: September 2009

10 9 8 7 6 5 4 3 2 1

Printed in the United States of America.

*I dedicate this book to my two adult children,
Kerri and Rick, who inquired frequently about
the status of this book;*

*my four grandchildren, Caroline, John, Maeve, and
Christopher, who bring much happiness and delight into
my life;*

*my siblings, Joyce, Charles, James, Earl (Sonny), and
Patricia (Patty), who often asked for a copy of this book;
and*

*lastly, to my wife, Annette, who for 39 years has provided
encouragement and inspiration.*

*A special thank you to Lynn Ash, who helped
tremendously on this book.*

Abstract

This book describes the role of the controller in a small business and provides a detailed "how-to" analysis of the many duties and responsibilities the small business controller often assumes. This work, based on approximately 30 years of working relationships with many small businesses, describes the functions many controllers of small businesses perform as well as specific elements they need to consider when performing specialized functions.

Keywords

Controllership, controller, small business

Contents

CHAPTER 1

Introduction

The Small Business Controller describes the role of the controller in a small business and provides a detailed "how-to" analysis of the various duties and responsibilities the controller often assumes. This work, based on approximately 30 years of working relationships with many small businesses, describes the functions many small business controllers perform as well as specific elements a controller needs to consider when performing specialized functions.

Chapter 1 outlines the content of each chapter and the transition from public accounting to private industry for the small business controller. Chapter 2 presents issues working with internal and external personnel, including the owner and dealing with outside professionals, such as legal advisors, outside CPA firms, banking relationships, information technology and computer consultants, and insurance agents and brokers. Chapter 2 concludes with comments regarding outsourcing and offshoring accounting and finance functions.

Chapter 3 includes the preparation of internal financial information and discusses relevant topics such as the information end user. Additionally, it presents key information about the quantity of information, its presentation, and content of the report. A discussion of financial ratios, including profitability, liquidity, leverage, and activity or turnover ratios is included. It also presents the fast close, along with suggestions on how to incorporate a fast close into the controller's role. Tables 3-1 through 3-3 and Figures 3-1 through 3-4 illustrate various key areas discussed within chapter 3.

Chapter 4 discusses a complete set of external financial statements and gives examples of compilation, review, and audit reports issued by outside accounting firms.

Chapter 5 presents the management of cash, including the importance of cash flow, the cash cycle, the cash conversion cycle, cash management and forecasting its cash position, investing idle cash, and compensating balances. Chapter 5 describes optimizing the float, including the collection and disbursement floats. Specific recommendations are part of this chapter to help increase the small business's cash flow. Tables 5-1 and 5-2 illustrate the various calculations and possible format for determining how to optimize the float.

Chapter 6 deals with the management of accounts receivable. Topics include the establishment of an effective credit policy, a financial analysis worksheet, and key financial ratios and the attainment of additional security on accounts receivable balances and a guarantee. It also discusses shortening the receivable cycle, accepting P-cards, and accounting for bad debts according to generally accepted accounting principles (GAAP) and the Internal Revenue Service (IRS). Table 6-1 presents a format to analyze accounts receivable over a prolonged period.

Chapter 7 discusses issues pertaining to the management of inventory, including inventory turnover, carrying costs, reorder points, different methods of inventory valuation, and the ABC approach. Additionally, it contains just-in-time inventory management, direct material and direct labor costs, and cycle counting. Table 7-1 illustrates a format emphasizing the impact that carrying costs and inventory levels have on cash and profits.

Chapter 8 discusses short-term financial planning, including the need for additional working capital, managing accounts payable, A, B, & C vendors, company commitment agreements, certificates of insurance, sales and use tax exemption certificates, and the Uniform Commercial Code (UCC) and security agreements. Additionally, it includes inventory returns and restocking charges. Table 8-1 presents a worksheet to use in the analysis of accounts payable.

Property, plant, and equipment, including the role of the controller in capital investment decisions, and investment evaluation methods including payback, net present value, and internal rate of return methods are part of chapter 9.

Chapter 10 discusses key points when raising capital and planning the capital structure and includes the cost of capital for debt and equity, cost of retained earnings, weighted-average cost of capital, financial leverage, hurdle rates, and treasury stock. Tables 10-1 and 10-2 illustrate specific relevant information.

Planning and budgeting are the topics in chapter 11. It includes the role of the controller in planning and budgeting, the break-even point, margin of safety, free cash flow, and fixed expenses and cost coverage ratio. We discuss static and flexible budgets and present lease versus debt financing. Tables 11-1 and 11-2 illustrate the importance of this internal information.

Chapter 12 contains topics on obtaining financing and increasing cash flow. Internal sources of financing, including reduction of inventory levels, profits, increasing accounts receivable collections, and accounts payable disbursement policies, are part of this chapter. We also discuss funding from shareholders, family, and friends, in addition to venture capitalists and angel investors. Tables 12-1 through 12-5 illustrate key points within this chapter.

Chapter 13 contains taxes for small businesses. We discuss key areas such as choice of entity—sole proprietorships, partnerships, C and S corporations, and limited liability companies (LLCs). Additionally, we present change in fiscal years, differences in net income and taxable income, deferred tax assets and tax liabilities, and permanent and temporary timing differences. This chapter also contains a discussion of the preparation and filing of Form 1099 and other information tax returns, the Alternative Minimum Tax (AMT), taking money out of S and C corporations, and preparing for an IRS audit. Lastly, it contains topics including debt versus equity financing by shareholders, tax planning strategies, and tax administrative matters.

Chapter 14 pertains to internal controls within the small business. It discusses the controller's role in internal controls, a definition and value of internal controls, and the development of an internal control structure. We present information regarding the overall responsibility for internal controls, including limitations of internal controls.

The changing role of the controller is part of chapter 15. Topics include professional and trade associations, ethics and ethical challenges, and the need for a small business code of ethics. We also discuss various professional accounting associations' code of ethics.

In today's environment, the controller for a small business often works without an adequate job description outlining all duties and responsibilities. They should have all the answers and are seldom able to accomplish all of their day-to-day activities without the help of an experienced and dedicated staff, which seldom is available.

Many definitions exist as to what constitutes a small business. Some organizations define small businesses by sales volume and number of employees. Others use different criteria, such as number of locations, customers, or suppliers. For example, Wikipedia defines small businesses in the United States as consisting of fewer than 100 employees, and are usually privately owned corporations, partnerships, or sole proprietors.[1] In this book, we adopt this definition to define small businesses. Regardless of the definition, it is important to note that the functions of the controller will vary greatly depending on many factors.

Regardless of how large or small the business, one key ingredient that all controllers must possess is the ability to analyze information. This ability might include the capacity to understand various ratios, spot trends, or understand the implication both the ratios and trends indicate for the company and the industry. Additionally, the technical knowledge the small business controller must possess is significant and includes the required rules and regulations necessary to prepare and present accurate financial information.

Whatever the job description of the small business controller, if there is a job description at all, it is reasonable to assume that neither is it all-inclusive nor does it identify accurately the total responsibility controllers possess within the organization. The controller of a small business usually does not have all of the talent and expertise readily available and usually seeks other alternatives.

Transition From Public Accounting to Private Industry

Many controllers for nonpublic companies transition from public accounting, whether it be from a "Big Four" firm or a smaller local firm. In public accounting, the individual may have been in an assurance and compliance role. Now in a small business environment, the individual may be moving into an area of management accounting and becoming a key player in management.

The transition from working in public accounting to private industry as a controller for a small business challenges the new controller to develop a new set of professional skills. While an individual working in public accounting acquires and develops many skills, the new small business controller may not have learned or developed many of the skills relevant to a position in private industry. Interpersonal, organizational, and supervisory expectations all demand a different set of skills and talents that require time and a different work setting to develop. For example, in large specialized public accounting firms, advance planning for meetings usually occurs, allowing the individual time to prepare. In private industry, however, there tends to be less time for controllers to make decisions. There are more demands for the controller's attention. There is an expectation of quick decisions. Employees look to the controller for direction and quick resolution of problems, not on a planned schedule. In general, the process moves faster, and decisions are expected quicker. This is indicative of the diverse job responsibilities and requirements of a small business controller.

Another transition challenge that the controller commonly encounters is the lack of a professional team. For example, in public accounting, a staff accountant typically will have access to individuals to discuss issues regarding a client. In small business, the support team often does not exist. As a result, the new controller needs to develop relationships with outside advisors and professionals who will be available when needed.

Now that you know about the contents of this book, let's move into chapter 2.

CHAPTER 2

Working With Internal and External Personnel

This chapter discusses the small business controller's need for an orientation (honeymoon) period. It outlines some important considerations when working with internal personnel such as the owner and board of directors. Additionally, it discusses a necessary relationship between the controller and external personnel such as legal advisors, outside CPA firms, bankers, information technology and computer consultants, and insurance agents and brokers. Lastly, we conclude this chapter with some issues regarding outsourcing and offshoring activities.

The Orientation (Honeymoon) Period

The controller must develop an attitude and image of being an integral part of the management team. He or she must portray an image of leadership and communicate accordingly. The controller utilizes this period to communicate effectively with the owner and put himself or herself in the owner's place when presenting information for the owner to consider. Get to know what "pushes his or her button," and understand how the controller can use this knowledge to be more proactive rather than reactive. For example, does the owner know how to read computer printouts, or do they just want a one-page recap? What is the best way to present the financial information to the owner each month? Is he very concerned about conserving cash, or does he want to measure return on investment? Armed with this kind of knowledge, the controller can utilize his strengths and other skills to ensure the owner is getting the kind of information he or she can understand and use appropriately.

The controller must also meet the needs of key managers. The controller needs to take an active interest in all departments and assist them whenever possible, regardless of the task or time commitment. This manner of cooperation may provide an opportunity for the controller to become a respected and knowledgeable ally for solving problems. Discuss with key managers the type of information they are currently receiving, if they understand it, and how they would like to see it improved to provide better and more relevant information. Keep the reports accurate and timely. Do not give key managers too much information, but rather keep the reports simple and clear.

When the controller asks the key managers how they can help them, some may be very vocal and challenging. Be prepared to listen. Do not react immediately, but rather digest the information for future use. The controller may sense a conflict between different managers, and if so, the controller should not make an immediate suggestion for resolution. Instead, he or she should gather all information and make an informed judgment later on how he can better serve everyone.

Working With the Owner

The controller must interact effectively with the owner, who may also be the chief executive officer (CEO). The owner has many areas of responsibility, as does the controller; thus, whenever the two meet, efficient use of time must occur. Current information is crucial for the business owner and includes all aspects of the business, including its financial challenges.

Once the controller determines how he will communicate with the owner, it must be timely and effective. Sometimes a face-to-face meeting is not always possible. It is important, however, that some form of communication, whether it is voice mail, e-mail, or information left in his or her office, takes place regularly.

Part of this communication process should include the type and amount of information the owner needs and understands. Several different ways are available to present the same financial information, and it is necessary for the controller to understand the strengths and shortcomings of the owner's understanding of the information. Some owners may be reluctant to convey their shortcomings, but an observant controller can usually tell when the information generated has not conveyed the intended meaning. If this continues to happen regularly, a revision of the information, as well as perhaps its presentation, may be necessary. Regardless of the type and amount of information, it is crucial that the communication process between the owner and the controller takes place regularly and that the time together is productive.

Working With the CEO and Other Executives on the Board of Directors

Dealing with a CEO or other executives on the board of directors may present additional challenges for the controller. For example, the CEO and other executives may be concerned about clear lines of authority or agreed upon priorities more than the owner. Different members of the board may have different priorities, and the controller may be the person to ensure that the requests of the CEO and other board members become realized. The process of dealing with the board may be formal, requiring written minutes and approval before any action. Each board member has a different personality, which requires the controller to become aware of, and satisfy, the learning styles of each member.

Dealing With Outside Professionals

Every business organization, whether small or large, public or private, must deal with outside professionals. The small business controller usually is part of the process that determines the need for outside professionals and where to locate them. Other employees in the organization may also need to work with outside professionals; thus, the controller communicates to employees the process and trains them on how to work effectively with outside professionals.

The controller usually prepares or reviews contracts pertaining to outside professionals. These contracts should be clear about the type of services and hourly rates. Many different outside professionals can be used effectively and efficiently by a small business if both parties have clearly defined expectations and outcomes.

Legal Advisors

Because of today's litigious environment, every business organization needs to have available outside legal representation. The controller must know when to contact an attorney and who provides the kind of services needed for different situations.

The controller, and perhaps other members of the management team, determines the needed legal services when dealing with attorneys. It is common to have a general business attorney for the initial contact outside the organization, as the controller often does not know how to proceed when legal situations arise. The general business attorney should have a significant knowledge of the industry within which the company operates and be able to determine the legal needs of the organization, which includes referring the company to other legal specialists when necessary. A good general business attorney will be able to offer many services, including, but not limited to, providing contracts, leases, company minute books, policies and procedures manuals, and advice on resolving issues pertaining to personnel matters.

As a relationship is formed with an outside general business attorney, it is necessary to be very specific as to hourly rates and expenses and whom within your company will be the contact person. Whatever assistance controllers, or their staff, can provide should help reduce the overall legal fees.

Outside CPA Firms

Although the controller may be a Certified Public Accountant (CPA) or a Certified Management Accountant (CMA) or hold some other professional designation, utilizing the services of an outside CPA firm is common. The company may require a financial audit, need help with the year-end federal and state corporation tax returns, or have other specific needs such as bonding or special-purpose financial statements required by major creditors or banks.

When dealing with outside CPA firms, it is important to obtain an engagement letter. The letter should outline the scope of the work, responsibilities, and cost of the engagement. Usually the CPA firm will prepare these automatically, and the controller often receives some comfort by having the agreement in writing.

If the controller is planning for an audit by an outside CPA firm, advance planning is necessary as to who will prepare what schedules so that both parties will complete everything in a timely manner. The controller and a person on the audit team with the CPA firm should agree on who will be the contact person from each organization, and all information should flow through these two people. Otherwise, chaos may develop and no one person is controlling the quality and quantity of information from each side.

It is common for the controller to talk with, and perhaps interview, several accounting firms to get a better understanding of the services provided and comparable fees. Sometimes the controller may feel that a different type of expertise is necessary than what is currently being provided. For example, if the controller determines that the business needs someone from an outside CPA firm who is knowledgeable in business succession, the controller will seek out that kind of expertise. When interviewing CPA firms, ask for references, who will actually service your account, and what different level of fees will be charged for varying levels of services.

Banking Relationships

Even though the relationship with a banker is usually not in contract form except for the loan documents themselves, it is a very important relationship. Rarely can an organization grow and prosper without the help and relationship of a financial institution. The professional relationship with its banker is one that can provide many opportunities as a company changes. For example, the line of credit that most companies have changes, as do interest rates and collateral for the line of credit and other outstanding obligations. In some special cases, owners and shareholders remove or alter personal guarantees. The negotiation of specific rates for special services from the bank may occur as the relationship develops. It is common for bankers to recommend a specific company buy products or services from other banking customers.

Do not underestimate the importance of this relationship. There are several ways to nourish this relationship: planning periodic lunches or events, getting to know the personnel who work in the bank or the branch where the organization banks, and keeping the banker apprised of any significant changes in the financial situation of the company. A friendly periodic phone call does not take much time, but the results may be quite significant.

Information Technology (IT) and Computer Consultants

IT needs are ever changing, and it is important to have someone available on a consulting basis to help with situations pertaining to the organization's technology.

The type of assistance the small business controller may require from an IT consultant can range from training of staff on software updates to recommending a new computer system. The consultant must be familiar with the type of software the organization uses and know how to repair the hardware when trouble arises.

Regardless of the current needs of the organization, it is important to select carefully the consultant based on his or her expertise and hourly rates. The agreement should be in writing, specifying hourly rates, overtime rates, if any, and expected response time. A good source of IT specialists is through local educational systems, such as high schools, colleges, and universities. Many consultants sponsor seminars and are guest speakers at business functions throughout the business community. A telephone call to the IT department of local academic institutions will probably give the controller several names of qualified consultants able to provide the necessary services. Before making a final decision, interview thoroughly and ask for references. Verify all references before making any commitment to the consultant.

Insurance Agents and Brokers

Every company needs a good risk-management program, and in many cases, the controller is responsible for this task. A new small business controller may not possess the expertise to recommend or implement the kind of changes that may be necessary to manage the risk effectively.

Thus, an outside insurance agent or broker who is familiar with the insurance market and understands the needs of the small business can be an integral part of the outside consulting team.

The controller needs to become knowledgeable in the insurance arena, review the various policies to make sure adequate coverage is obtained, and prepare a spreadsheet analysis of the trends in both the type and amount of coverage, as well as the costs and losses incurred over the last 5-year period.

Good communication between the controller and the insurance agent or broker is necessary to make sure the potential exposure of assets and other areas is minimal. Usually there is no outside contract to sign with insurance brokers or agents.

Outsourcing and Offshoring Various Accounting Functions or Information

Many internally provided accounting functions could be outsourced. Outsourcing is the external completion of previous internal functions, whereas offshoring is the moving of some function to another country. Regardless of the process chosen, the controller needs to thoroughly review the internal functions of the organization and provide input into the decision to outsource or offshore specific functions.

Outsourcing can provide seasonal labor without the expense of permanent employees, which can be especially beneficial to companies that have big changes in its business cycle. Some significant cost reductions can be achieved by outsourcing, as sometimes outsourced labor is less expensive. On the downside, make sure the liability insurance coverage of an organization provides for risks associated with outsourcing.

Although some of the day-to-day functions the controller's staff previously provided may have been outsourced, the controller is still responsible for the overall quality of information generated and subsequently provided to managers and owners. The controller should be involved in any outsourcing or offshoring activities, as they may be more knowledgeable about the transition and financial problems associated with the activity.

Just about any function within an organization can be outsourced or offshored. Outsourcing and offshoring can provide the controller with more time to devote to other areas, if used and monitored properly. Companies need to consider the environmental risks and social responsibility attached to outsourcing and offshoring, in addition to the hidden costs that may offset any projected savings. For example, the change in the currency value from one country to another over time could require a company to hedge its potential losses by putting caps on currency fluctuations.

As noted previously in this chapter, a small business controller must communicate effectively with internal owners, the board of directors, and managers. Additionally, the controller is an integral part of the process of selecting and controlling the use of outside professionals. Finally, outsourcing and offshoring can be used effectively by small businesses if it is handled properly.

Chapter 3 discusses the preparation of internal financial information as well as its relevancy to the information end user.

CHAPTER 3

Preparation of Internal Financial Information

This chapter presents several topics, including internal financial information, which address such issues as the users of the financial information, the quantity of information, the presentation of the information, and the content of an internal report. Additionally, this chapter contains financial ratios, including examples of profitability, liquidity, financial leverage, activity (turnover) ratios, and the fast close. Lastly, we introduce three tables to illustrate the types of reports often provided to internal management.

Internal Financial Information

Many controllers of small businesses understand that the responsibility to provide timely and relevant information to decision makers does not end with the preparation of monthly financial statements. The controller must be proactive in his approach to identify certain trends, positive or otherwise, in addition to presenting information that will add credibility and relevance to the situation.

Traditionally, presenting internal financial information meant preparing and distributing reports regarding past performance. Often this information left management without the relevant information necessary to help plan how the company would meet its goals. However, internal reporting does not have to reflect only past performance. Internal reports are an important tool to allow management to focus on current and future needs of the organization.

The amount, quality, and timeliness of the information, both financial and other, depend on the needs of the users. As business conditions change, and as other important needs of the company change, the controller must be flexible enough to make whatever changes are necessary to report the information in a meaningful way. For example, one month the controller may emphasize a problem with trade accounts receivable and perhaps show charts or graphs of how it has increased. Other times, a computer printout may suffice.

A small business controller should understand who is using the information prepared by his office. Different levels within the organization (e.g., top management versus middle management) will have different needs and understanding capabilities. The overall understanding of the user will help the controller adjust the amount of detail, adding credibility and perhaps supporting details to the financial information. Another service the controller provides is to train users, either individually or as a group, on how to understand the information.

The controller, when preparing the internal financial information, should consider the following factors.

The Information End User[1]

Many different users have need for financial information from the controller. For example, some users of financial information often include the following (not listed in any specific order of importance):

- *Shareholders, investors, or both.* These types of users often use the information for making investment decisions about holding, buying additional shares, or selling shares of stock in the corporation. Additionally, the shareholders may have a fiduciary responsibility, such as serving on committees of the small business. They may attempt to project profits and cash flows based on recent trends and future financial information, or both.
- *Managers.* This group may be the most important internal user of information. Not only are they involved in the day-to-day decision-making process that occurs within the organization, but they may also be involved in incentive contracts for others within the organization (i.e., bonuses based on some level of accomplished performance). Additionally, they may receive funding for long-term projects based on various financial ratios described in this book. Managers also use the information to change the direction of the company, based on profit margins

per product line or other specific areas defined by organizational goals and measurement standards.

- *Lenders and other suppliers.* One of the major lenders within a small business are banks. Part of the required letter of commitment signed by owners of the small business often specifies various financial performances, such as a certain amount of net income per year increasing retained earnings of the corporation or, more commonly, requiring specific ratios and other covenants. It is common for the bank to require a specific working capital ratio (current assets divided by current liabilities) at the end of the business's fiscal year. Major creditors who extend credit to customers may also request a copy of internal financial statements periodically, as well as require reviewed or audited year-end financial statements.
- *Employees.* The financial information that is generated for employees may indicate solvency of the business and the viability of pension contributions and the safety of those previously received.
- *Government regulatory agencies.* The list of government regulators is exhausting and far-reaching. For example, the Internal Revenue Service and State Department of Revenue agencies want to ensure the proper reporting of income and expenses for tax purposes. Often they will require a reconciliation of net income per financial statements to taxable income per tax returns.

Because the users of the financial information have different purposes and interests, some users often express concerns about the source of the information and what it means. This often presents a conflict. For example, it is common for the bank extending a loan to finance the acquisition of a vehicle to want the repayment over a short period of time (e.g., 3 years). However, from a cash flow standpoint, the business may want to repay the loan over a longer period (e.g., 4 years) to conserve cash.

The Quantity of Information

As noted previously, the controller needs to be able to synthesize information and determine its importance to each group within the organization, and as such, he generates and presents information that focuses management on the issues. For example, executive management may require focused, highly summarized reports that emphasize unusual or exceptional performance. Conversely, middle management might prefer more operational details covering specific parts of the organization. The controller should consider distributing the financial information through the company intranet, if available and proper controls are in place. Utilizing specialized software can tailor the information to the individual needs of each user. In some cases, a one-page report may be all that is necessary on a periodic basis to highlight certain relevant areas. For example, Table 3-1 pertains to trade accounts receivable. This one-page report summarizes how trade accounts receivable has changed from June 30, 2009, through August 31, 2009. Upon review, the user can determine the increase in trade accounts receivable over this 2-month period ($443,000) and also the change in the mix of accounts receivable between the different categories (current, 1–30 days past due, etc.). Armed with this information, management can focus on why the changes occurred and take corrective action.

Regardless of the presentation of the information, the controller asks the users to provide feedback regarding the content of the report(s) and what changes they might recommend to present information that is more

Table 3-1. Accounts Receivable—Trade (in Thousands)

	Total	Current	1–30 days past due	31–60 days past due	61–90 days past due	Over 90 days past due
As of June 30, 2009	1,220	986	95	64	45	30
% of total receivables	100%	81%	8%	5%	4%	2%
As of July 31, 2009	1,445	1,105	156	48	67	69
% of total receivables	100%	76%	11%	3%	5%	5%
As of August 31, 2009	1,663	1,207	228	145	42	41
% of total receivables	100%	73%	14%	9%	2%	2%

meaningful. This exchange of information may provide valuable feedback for the controller as to formatting future reports, as well as providing users with the kind of information they understand.

The Presentation of the Information

Not only should the quantity and quality of information be a consideration for the controller, but also the presentation of the information may be a major concern. People learn and understand information differently. Some may like the format of traditional financial statements with columns and rows, while others like to see charts and graphs, and still others understand words better, which complement charts and graphs as well as traditional rows and columns. For example, the controller might attach a cover sheet or memo to the periodic reports that highlights important results or trends. Table 3-2 provides an example of an important result and trend that the controller would want to emphasize.

Additionally, inexpensive software packages produce different types of charts (pie, line, and bar) and may be able to communicate better than words and traditional financial information.

Many companies use flash reports, which contain specific information in recap form rather than presenting a lot of irrelevant information or detracting from the purpose of the report. Table 3-3 provides an example of presenting information in recap form.

Table 3-2. Highlighting Important Trends or Results

	3 months ended 6/30/2008 ($)	%	3 months ended 6/30/2009 ($)	%
Sales	1,155,600	100	1,200,350	100
Cost of sales	809,000	70	816,000	68
Gross profit	346,600	30	384,350	32
Operating expenses	213,000	18	215,000	18
Net income before taxes	133,600	12	169,350	14

Memo From Controller to All Users: While reviewing Table 3-2, please notice the change in the cost of sales section of the income statement. Our sales volume is about $45,000 higher than the same period in 2008, but more importantly, we were able to increase the gross profit percentage by 2 points during the same period in 2009.

Table 3-3. An Example of a Flash Report Comparison for June 30, 2007 Through 2009

	2007	2008	2009
Cash in bank ($)	67,000	43,500	31,400
Accounts receivable—trade—gross ($)	2,150,000	2,420,000	2,573,000
Inventory ($)	1,573,000	1,643,000	1,803,000
Accounts payable—trade ($)	1,571,000	1,745,000	1,963,000
Accrued liabilities ($)	623,000	583,000	437,000

Another means of communicating the information is through presentation software, such as PowerPoint. Whatever method the controller chooses to communicate the information, evidence has shown that an effective report depends on the information contained in the report, as well as its overall appearance.

The Content of the Report

Once the controller identifies the use of the information, his accounting and business expertise helps in determining what information to put in the report. The information should be accurate, timely, understandable, and emphasized or highlighted.

Accurate

The information should contain no mathematical or typographical errors. The controller should review each word to make sure it conveys the intended message before distributing it to other management personnel. If some information contained in the report is unverified, the report should clearly state that the item is subject to review and further updates will be forthcoming. The controller gains a significant amount of credibility by generating accurate, meaningful information.

Timely

The controller needs to produce timely information. Outdated or stale information is meaningless in most cases; thus, the controller should ascertain that the information is available within the previously established period.

Understandable

Keep the reports simple and easy to read, as the controller is communicating a message. The controller should ascertain that the user received the information and has access to additional detail if necessary. As noted previously, different formats and different methods of presenting the information may make the information more understandable to different users.

Emphasized or Highlighted

The controller may wish to emphasize or highlight specific parts or portions of the information. This may be to create a thorough and exhaustive review, or perhaps the controller wants to call the reader's attention to some very specific points. The controller may also use asterisks or other methods to accomplish this purpose.

If some of the information is forward-looking (prospective), such as budgets, forecasts, and projections, communicate the assumptions used to prepare the documents. Supporting documentation should also be available to anyone who needs it. Internal information has its limitations, and the information presented becomes much more meaningful when the users understand its preparation and intended purpose.

Financial Ratios

Even before the controller starts comparing his current financial information with past periods, top management determines what measurable areas they want to monitor. Specific ratios have more meaning when compared to change over a period of time as well as other companies within the same industry; however, depending on the industry, the specific ratios may or may not be important. Many different ratios are available; however, to be concise, I have listed the most relevant below.

The following ratios are profitability, liquidity, leverage, and activity functions. Each group has specific calculations and explanations as to what each function and individual ratios mean.

Profitability Ratios

These types of ratios pertain to the firm's ability to generate a profit. The four ratios include the return on sales ratio, the gross profit ratio, the return on stockholders' equity ratio, and the return on total assets ratio.

1. *Net income/net sales.* This is the return on sales ratio. It measures how much net income comes from each dollar of net sales. This percentage will vary significantly from industry to industry; thus, it is important to monitor any changes on a consistent basis.
2. *Net sales less cost of goods sold/net sales.* This is called the gross profit ratio and measures the gross profit generated by each dollar of net sales. This ratio changes as a change in the cost structure occurs or with additional competition.
3. *Net income/average stockholders' equity.* This ratio is the return on stockholders' equity, and it is the first of the three ratios introduced thus far that considers a balance sheet item—the average stockholders' equity. Although this ratio may not be as important for small businesses, it measures the percentage of return provided to its shareholders during the year.
4. *Net income/average total assets.* This last ratio under the profitability group of ratios is the return on total assets. It measures how efficiently the business has utilized its assets to produce net income. (Note: This author recommends reducing total assets by any intangible assets that may be on the balance sheet before calculating this ratio.)

Figure 3-1. Illustration of Key Profitability Financial Ratios

Liquidity Ratios

Liquidity ratios pertain to items contained on the balance sheet and measure an organization's ability to meet its short-term debt when due. These types of ratios are perhaps more important than some of the others because they identify potential cash flow problems and the inability to pay creditors when payment is due.

Leverage Ratios

This third set of ratios measures how the business is financing its assets. In other words, the higher the ratios, the greater the financing provided by creditors.

1.   *Current assets/current liabilities.* This is the current ratio and measures the extent of current assets as compared to current liabilities. Historically, again depending on the industry, a 2 to 1 ratio has been considered to be the norm; however, economic and other conditions have altered this somewhat. Generally, the larger this ratio, the more liquid the company.
2.   *Cash plus short-term marketable plus accounts receivable (net)/current liabilities.* This is the quick ratio or the acid-test ratio, and it calculates the "quick assets" (those excluding inventory and prepaid expenses) ability to pay off the current liabilities that become due. This can be significantly different from the current ratio presented previously because of the exclusion of the inventory as part of the numerator. Historically, this ratio is adequate when 1 to 1; however, it varies greatly from industry to industry.

Figure 3-2. Illustration of Key Liquidity Ratios

1. *Total liabilities/stockholders' equity.* This is the debt to equity ratio and is used to measure the relationship of creditors to shareholders. Creditors generally like to see this ratio no greater than .50 to 1, indicating possibly few problems with repayment when due.
2. *Long-term debt/stockholders' equity.* This ratio is the long-term debt to equity and excludes the current liabilities from its numerator. Its purpose is to determine what percentage of assets long-term creditors are financing. This ratio may impact interest rates on future borrowings.

Figure 3-3. Illustration of Key Leverage Ratios

Activity (or Turnover) Ratios

The last set of financial ratios are the activity or turnover ratios. These ratios determine how efficiently the company utilizes its assets (resources).

The Fast Close

The monthly closing process of the general ledger accounts in anticipation of preparing internal financial statements is often a stressful and time-consuming process for many small businesses. The controller probably will have to interrupt normal daily activities to supervise or participate significantly in generating accurate and timely financial information. The controller must take a leadership role to assure that the type and amount of financial information is generated as quickly and accurately as possible after the month ends.

The controller assesses critically and objectively each function of the closing process, determining how to decrease the amount of time needed to close the books without materially affecting the quality of the information. Some ways to reduce the closing time follow.

Preparation of a Full Set of Financial Statements Only Each Quarter

Many companies are realizing the expense and time for the accounting department to prepare a complete set of financial statements on a monthly

1. *Total charge sales/average accounts receivable (net).* This calculation is the accounts receivable turnover and measures how efficiently the business is collecting its accounts receivable. The relationship shown in this calculation illustrates how long it takes to collect accounts receivable.

2. *365/accounts receivable turnover.* This ratio is the day's sales in accounts receivable and measures how long it takes from the initial sale to convert the receivable into cash. This calculation is related to the accounts receivable turnover ratio presented previously. This ratio measures how the credit department collects its receivables. This turnover often reflects cash flow and/or the inability to pay obligations when due.

3. *Cost of goods sold/average inventory.* This is called the inventory turnover ratio, and it indicates the number of times the inventory turns over during the year. It measures how the business is managing its investment in inventory. Please notice that the calculation compares the cost of sales to the cost of inventory (costs vs. costs). Some analysts suggest using the selling price as the numerator; however, this author disagrees. This is an important ratio for any business that sells inventory, and it should be compared carefully with other small businesses in the same industry, using the same inventory valuation method.

4. *365/inventory turnover.* This is the day's sales in inventory turnover, and it is very similar to the inventory turnover ratio discussed previously. This is another important comparison, as it indicates how many day's sales of inventory is on hand. Being overstocked or understocked (stockouts, etc.) may indicate some hidden problems that can affect the viability of the organization. This will be discussed further in a later section.

Figure 3-4. Illustration of Key Activity (or Turnover) Ratios

basis. Because of this, many companies have changed to preparing only specific key items or statistics each month, and then preparing a complete set of financial statements at the end of each quarter. Many variations of the type and amount of monthly financial information are available. Before the controller suggests this significant change, they should thoroughly investigate suggested changes, the type of financial information presented each month with specific examples, and an estimated amount of how much time and expense the company may save.

Selection of Four 13-Week Periods

To increase the comparability of the same reporting period (4 weeks in this case), some companies have selected thirteen 28-day closing cycles, rather than the traditional 12 monthly closings. The advantage to this method is that a uniform closing date (such as every fourth Friday) occurs. Additionally, this process might significantly reduce some of the normal adjusting entries made each month. Before changing to this method, the controller ascertains when the normal monthly recurring expenses such as rent, utilities, and insurance, just to name a few, are incurred or disbursed. However, the change to this type of closing system may create other unexpected problems that may override the efficiencies previously expected.

An Article by the Institute of Management and Administration

The Accounting Department Management Report (ADMR) reviewed a joint presentation by SAP and PricewaterhouseCoopers and suggested various ways to improve the closing process.[2] Some specific conclusions from the study are as follows:

1. Leading companies in all four industry sectors presented (manufacturing; consumer products; energy and telecom; and finance, insurance, health care, and nonprofit) were able to close in 1 day, as compared to a high of 6 to 10 days.
2. The work hours to complete the close were significantly different by industry. For example, the energy and telecom industry showed

a minimum of 72 hours to close, as compared to the average of 553 hours.

3. The following are some of the best practices found in the study:

   a. Intelligent use of estimates and accruals. ADMR found that many companies do not use monthly accruals and estimates, but rather report them in the following month.

   b. The automation or elimination of manual entries.

   c. The identification and elimination of non-value-added activities. ADMR suggests recording such things as amortization and depreciation quarterly rather than monthly.

   d. Establishment of materiality thresholds. Once these thresholds have been established, anything above them can be investigated and adjusted as necessary.

   e. Clear outlining of duties, responsibilities, and deadlines for personnel responsible for the closing process. Additionally, these people should be cross-trained.

A Report by ADMR

A 2004 report by ADMR states that the financial staff spends approximately 80% of its time each month on activities such as closing the books and essential balancing and reconciliation functions.[3] Controllers, whether public or private, are always searching for ways to reduce this overall cost as well as produce more timely and meaningful financial information.

This chapter reviewed the different techniques used to present accurate, timely, and meaningful internal information. Three tables illustrated and presented the use of different formats and purposes of internal information. Specific financial ratios, including profitability, liquidity, leverage, and activity (turnover), were calculated and illustrated with four figures. Lastly, in this chapter, the fast close was discussed as well as various techniques to save time and expense in providing the required monthly internal information.

Chapter 4 discusses a complete set of external financial information and gives examples of compilation, review, and audit reports presented by outside accounting firms.

CHAPTER 4

A Complete Set of External Financial Statements

This chapter focuses on the preparation of a complete set of financial statements for external parties. We discuss the three distinct parts to external financial statements—the accountant's report, the four financial statements, and the notes. The chapter concludes with a discussion and illustrations of three distinct reports often prepared by outside CPA firms—compilations, reviews, and audits.

Three Distinct Parts to a Set of External Financial Statements

As noted in chapter 3, many users have different needs for financial statement information. Previously, mostly internal users of information were discussed; however, external users, such as bankers, major creditors, suppliers, and federal and state regulatory agencies, request, and in some cases require, an external financial statement that is acceptable in format and content in accordance with generally accepted accounting principles (GAAP).

A complete set of financial statements for external users consists of three distinct parts. First is the accountant's report describing what assurance relates to the accuracy of the financial statements presented and usually includes a compilation, review, or audit report issued by the accounting firm.

Second are the four basic financial statements. The first is the balance sheet (also called the statement of financial position or the statement of financial condition), which presents the company's financial position at a specific point in time, for example, December 31, 2009. It includes a listing of all assets (things of value to the business), all liabilities (debts and obligations to be repaid to creditors), and net worth or stockholders' equity (what is left or who owns the rest of the assets listed, also called residual value).

The income statement appears next, and it contains how much net profit or net loss the company generated over a specified period, such as 1 month, 3 months, or 1 year. An example would be an income statement presented for "Twelve Months Ended December 31, 2009." This financial statement is a cumulative amount over a period, not to exceed 1 year. It contains all income (things that have been earned), expenses (costs incurred to generate the income presented on this income statement), and the difference between the two figures. If income exceeds all expenses, the residual is net income. If expenses exceed income, it is a net loss.

The third financial statement usually presented is the statement of cash flows. It converts the income and expenses reported on the income statement to the amount received and disbursed in cash. One of the purposes of this statement is to complement and supplement the income statement and balance sheet. Three distinct sections appear in the statement of cash flows—operating, investing, and financing. The individual three sections of the statement allow the reader of the financial information the ability to determine which source (operating, investing, and financing) generated or used the most cash.

The final financial statement is usually the statement of retained earnings. A corporation uses the retained earnings statement and shows how that account changed from the beginning to the end of the year. Although several items affect the retained earnings, it is sufficient to understand that retained earnings increases by profitable operations (net income) and decreases by unprofitable operations (net losses) and dividends. Thus, the general formula for the statement of retained earnings is the beginning of the period balance (i.e., January 1, 2009) plus the net income for the year (12 months ended December 31, 2009) or less net loss for the same period, less dividend declared to shareholders, equals the retained earnings at end of period (i.e., December 31, 2009).

The last section of a complete set of financial statements includes the notes to the financial statements. This section describes the accounting policies and accounting estimates used in the financial statements, and often includes many important items or comments that may affect future profits and cash flow. These notes are very relevant for a complete understanding of the financial statements.

Compilation, Review, and Audit Financial Statement Services Offered by Accounting Firms

Most public accounting firms offer many types of services to small businesses, depending on the needs of the specific client. As the small business controller, they understand the difference between the various levels of standards the public accounting firm must adhere to depending on the type of services provided.

Most every organization, whether public or nonpublic, profit or nonprofit, must in some way prepare a report on its financial position and performance. The accounting profession has developed different types of standards, each with its own specific audience.

The public accounting firm provides three distinct services. Each service meets the specific needs of the client.

Compilation Services

This level of service involves preparing financial statements based on information provided by the organization's management. Small, privately held businesses may utilize this type of service monthly, quarterly, or annually. The accounting firm helps the organization prepare its financial statements. However, the accounting firm offers no assurance as to whether material, or significant, changes are necessary for the financial statements to conform to GAAP. During a compilation engagement, the accounting firm arranges the financial data into financial statement form. No investigation or searching occurs unless the accounting firm becomes aware the data provided are inaccurate or incomplete. The accounting firm expresses no opinion.

The current standards regarding compilation services allow the accounting firm to compile the financial information and omit the notes to the financial statements that are usually part of a complete set of financial statements. If management and the accounting firm select this type of omission, the standard report includes an additional paragraph stating that management has elected to omit the disclosures. This additional paragraph alerts the reader of the financial statements that if the financial statement contained the disclosures, it might affect the user's conclusions.

The standard compilation report is as follows:[1]

Accountant's Compilation Report

Stockholders and Board of Directors
ABC Company

We have compiled the accompanying balance sheet of ABC Company as of June 30, 2009, and the related statements of income, retained earnings, and cash flows for the year then ended, in accordance with Statements on Standards for Accounting and Review Services issued by the American Institute of Certified Public Accountants.

A compilation is limited to presenting in the form of financial statements information that is the representation of management (owners). We have not audited or reviewed the accompanying financial statements and, accordingly, do not express an opinion or any other form of assurance on them.

XYZ Accounting Firm
August 15, 2009

This type of report may be sufficient for many small businesses; however, if a business needs to provide some level of assurance that its financial statements are reliable, it may be necessary to have an outside accounting firm issue a review or an audit. A compilation is usually the lowest level of reporting service an accounting firm can provide, and the fees associated with this type of service are usually the lowest.

Review Services

The second level of financial reporting services that an outside accounting firm provides is a review. The reviewed financial statements may be appropriate for businesses that need to report their financial results to third parties, such as creditors and regulatory agencies.

The report issued by the accounting firm provides limited assurance that no material changes to the financial statements are necessary. The amount of assurance and reliability provided by the reviewed statements falls between compilations, discussed previously, which provide no assurance, and the audit, which provides a much higher level of assurance. It is still important to note that the reviewed statements are the representation of management, not the accounting firm. Management needs to have a sufficient understanding of the financial statements to assume responsibility for them.

The reviewed financial statements must include all notes to the financial statements, whereas in a compilation they sometimes are not included. Additionally, the accounting firm must remain independent during the review engagement. The review engagement requires the accounting firm to make specific inquiries of various matters, such as accounting principles and practices, record-keeping practices, accounting policies, actions of the board of directors, and changes in business activities. The accounting firm must apply some type of analytical procedures designed to identify unusual items or trends in the financial statements that may need additional explanation. Primarily, a review evaluates whether the financial statements are understandable and reliable without applying various tests that an audit requires.

A review does not require the accounting firm to confirm balances with banks or creditors, observe the physical inventory, or test selected transactions by examining supporting documents. However, in many cases, a review, which contains limited assurance, may be appropriate for a business or its creditors.

The standard review report is as follows:[2]

Accountant's Review Report

Stockholders and Board of Directors
ABC Company

We have reviewed the accompanying balance sheet of ABC Company as of June 30, 2009, and the related statements of income, retained earnings, and cash flows for the year then ended, in accordance with Statements on Standards for Accounting and Review Services issued by the American Institute of Certified Public Accountants. All information included in these financial statements is the representation of the management (owners) of ABC Company.

A review consists principally of inquiries of company personnel and analytical procedures applied to financial data. It is substantially less in scope than an audit in accordance with generally accepted auditing standards, the objective of which is the expression of an opinion regarding the financial statements taken as a whole. Accordingly, we do not express such an opinion.

Based on our review, we are not aware of any material modifications that should be made to the accompanying financial statements in order for them to be in conformity with generally accepted accounting principles.

XYZ Accounting Firm
August 15, 2009

If a review does not provide the level of assurance needed, the business may need an audit.

Audit Services

Some private companies may be required to engage an outside accounting firm to audit its financial statements and issue a report providing the highest level of assurance that the financial statements presents fairly in conformity with GAAP. During an audit, the accountant gathers evidence regarding the reliability of the financial statements. The accountant generally confirms balances with banks and creditors, observes the counting of the physical inventory, and tests selected documents external to the organization to gather information that may be more objective than internal documents. For example, by obtaining written confirmation from the client's customers of the amounts owed to the client as of a specific date, the accountant attempts to reduce the risk that the financial statements will be materially incorrect. After all the information is verified, the accountant issues a report stating that the financial statements are presented fairly, in all material respects, in conformity with GAAP. The audit is planned and performed with an attitude of professional skepticism, which means that the auditor is required to design various tests of the accounting records that provide reasonable assurance that material errors or fraud are detected. However, not all types of fraud, if any, may be uncovered, if an auditor is untrained to find fraudulent behavior, or if customary audit procedures fail to detect this type of activity. Statement on Auditing Standards (SAS) 99,[3] *Consideration of Fraud in a Financial Statement Audit*, provides guidance to the CPA regarding the responsibility to detect fraud during an audit. Although the audit does provide some reasonable basis for a higher level of assurance that the financial statements do not contain material errors or fraud, an audit does not guarantee absolute assurance.

An illustrative audit report is as follows:[4]

Independent Auditor's Report

Stockholders and Board of Directors
ABC Company

We have audited the accompanying balance sheet of ABC Company as of June 30, 2009, and the related statements of income, retained earnings, and cash flows for the year then ended. These financial statements are the responsibility of the Company's management. Our responsibility is to express an opinion on these financial statements based on our audit.

We conducted our audit in accordance with auditing standards generally accepted in the United States of America. Those standards require that we plan and perform the audit to obtain reasonable assurance about whether the financial statements are free from material misstatement. An audit includes examining, on a test basis, evidence supporting the amounts and disclosures to the financial statements. An audit also includes assessing the accounting principles used and significant estimates made by management, as well as evaluating the overall financial statement presentation. We believe that our audit provides a reasonable basis for our opinion.

In our opinion, the financial statements referred to above present fairly, in all material respects, the financial position of ABC Company as of June 30, 2009, and the results of its operations and its cash flows for the year then ended in conformity with accounting principles generally accepted in the United States of America.

XYZ Accounting Firm
August 15, 2009

Regardless of what type of services the outside accounting firm is providing, it is important to obtain an engagement letter, specifying estimated fees, services to perform, timetable for completion, and services expected from the controller's staff.

In this chapter, we discussed a complete set of external financial statements and the necessity of having an independent accountant's report and the notes as an integral part of the four required financial statements. We presented illustrated examples of compilation, review, and audited financial reports often issued by an outside accounting firm.

The next chapter discusses the management of cash and many of the important issues pertaining to it.

CHAPTER 5

Management of Cash

This chapter discusses several issues pertaining to the management of cash, including the cash cycle and a definition and examples of the cash conversion cycle. We present the benefits of cash forecasting, in addition to different techniques to invest idle cash for a period of 30 days and beyond. We discuss compensating balances and lastly suggest several ways to optimize the collection and disbursement floats.

The Importance of Cash Flow

Some authors have suggested that cash flow is more important than net income for an organization. Although I do not agree with the generalities of the statement, every organization needs to generate an adequate amount of cash flow, and if surplus cash occurs periodically, it needs to earn a return that will increase net income.

The Cash Cycle

When calculating an organization's cash flow, many recommend starting with a couple of ratios. In chapter 3, I presented various key ratios, as well as a discussion outlining some specific limitations regarding ratio analysis. Ratio analysis is not an end in itself, even though some calculations are easy for several key ratios and if used properly can provide trends and predict potential problem areas. For example, one key ratio usually calculated is the current ratio, which is current assets divided by current liabilities. As noted previously, this ratio measures how liquid a company is and indicates current assets in relation to current liabilities. What is adequate depends on the specific industry in which the organization operates. As an example, an industry such as a service organization might consider a current ratio of 1 to 1 sufficient, whereas a manufacturing company within a specific growth industry might require a ratio of 2.5 to 1 or higher.

The quick ratio, also called the acid-test ratio, is often calculated. This calculation is similar to the current ratio; however, the numerator, which is total current assets for the current ratio, consists of only cash, short-term investments, and net accounts receivable. These three assets are very close to cash or easily converted to cash (e.g., factoring or selling trade accounts receivable). The numerator for the quick ratio excludes inventory, which is a large item for many organizations. Although inventory sales can occur in one large transaction, it does not have reasonably assured proceeds applicable to the sale of accounts receivable. Thus, it is not part of the numerator. The denominator is current liabilities, same as used in the current ratio. Industry figures should be obtained for similar ratios and a comparison made, because as noted previously, what may be considered adequate for one industry can vary significantly between different industries.

The controller often prepares various calculations and interprets the results for other management team members. He communicates to management and other interested parties that an organization that receives payment sooner for its products or services and pays later for its recurring expenses and inventory has a competitive advantage. For example, if a company receives payment for its sales up front (e.g., accepting credit cards or enticing early payment of the net invoice) and does not pay its suppliers and other trade vendors until 30 days later, a significant portion of its daily operations will be financed by its vendors and suppliers. A common technique used to measure this efficiency is the calculation of the cash conversion cycle.

Cash Conversion Cycle

Each company has a different cash conversion cycle, defined as the number of days an organization takes to convert a dollar of inventory into a dollar of sales. Generally, a lower cash conversion cycle is better than a higher one. Some companies even have negative numbers, which indicates that the business is converting its products into cash before it pays for its product or services.

The cash conversion cycle (CCC) calculation starts by determining the days sales in inventory (DSI), which is the number of days the inventory remains unsold. To this calculation, we add the days sales outstanding (DSO), which is the time customers take to pay for their merchandise or services, and then deduct the time we take to pay our suppliers or vendors, called the days purchases outstanding (DPO).[1] Table 5-1 presents an example of the information gathered, the calculations made, and the information generated to produce the CCC.

Based on the information contained in Table 5-1, the company's cash conversion cycle is 99 days. This means a dollar spent on goods sold by the organization converts to cash in 99 days. Although 99 days may appear to be a long time, the controller needs to review industry averages and make appropriate comparisons, in addition to reviewing trends over several years within the business. How can we lower the overall CCC?

Table 5-1. Cash Conversion Cycle (CCC)

Calculation of days inventory outstanding (DIO)	
Cost of goods sold for the year	$4,500,000
Cost of goods sold per day (annual cost of goods sold/365) ($4,500,000/365)	$12,329
Inventory at end of year	$1,600,000
DIO ($1,600,000/$12,329)	**130 days**
Calculation of days sales outstanding (DSO)	
Revenues for the year	$5,700,000
Revenues per day (annual revenues/365) ($5,700,000/365)	$15,617
Accounts receivable—trade at end of year	$850,000
DSO ($850,000/$15,617)	**54 days**
Calculation of days payable outstanding (DPO)	
Cost of goods sold for the year (from above)	$4,500,000
Cost of goods sold per day (from above)	$12,329
Accounts payable at end of year	$1,050,000
DPO (accounts payable/cost of goods sold per day) ($1,050,000/$12,329)	**85 days**
Company's cash conversion cycle (130 + 54 - 85 = 99)	**99 days**

Cash Management and Forecasting Its Cash Position

Regardless of how profitable a company is, or has been, all businesses need a sufficient amount of cash to pay its obligations in a timely manner. Even if a company has excess cash, the effective and efficient utilization of all available resources is important.

A significant item within the cash flow projections contained in the cash budget is an estimate of the collection process and the determination of how long it takes to collect cash from accounts receivables. Some accounting software packages include cash forecasting as part of the package or added for an additional fee. The controller should review what the company currently has available and see if software alterations can occur to meet their specific needs.

Investing Idle Cash

If a company is fortunate enough to have excess cash, it must produce the highest return possible for the time available, in addition to ensuring the risk and availability of the funds match the cash flow needs of the organization. A business must determine if the excess cash is available within the next 30 days or, if unavailable within the next 30 days, still readily available if conditions change.

Investing Cash Beyond 30 Days

If a company does not need the cash within the next 30 days, a typical course of action may be to reduce the outstanding line of credit (which is available again when needed) or to invest in low-risk certificates of deposit or treasury bills. The controller should check with an officer of the bank where it has a banking relationship to obtain current information.

Investing Idle Cash for Less Than 30 Days

Even if an organization has seasonal fluctuations in its cash flow and has excess cash for less than 30 days, this cash should still generate some income. Do not let the cash sit inactive and unproductive.

Compensating Balances

It is common when a business opens a line of credit for the bank to require a compensating balance agreement, which is a form of collateral or security. This means that the company is required to maintain a compensating cash balance in its checking or savings accounts equal to 10% to 20% of the total amount outstanding on the line of credit. When this situation occurs, the company is unable to utilize this required cash balance and the cash usually remains idle and unproductive. It is usual for a bank to eliminate the compensating balance requirement for other forms of collateral and guarantees.[2] The controller should review this situation with the banker. A company with idle cash has many investment alternatives. Some investments require 1 year, while others only a few days. The various investment possibilities are beyond the scope of this book.

There is very little risk in investing cash on a short-term basis; however, the cash must be available when needed. Some usual investments noted previously do not allow the money to be withdrawn until the maturity date. For example, if the money is unavailable for 10 days, and because of unexpected circumstances, the cash becomes needed in 3 days, it may not be available at all or perhaps unavailable without paying a penalty.

Optimizing the Float

A controller can "optimize the float" by understanding and improving the collection float and the disbursement float.

The Collection Float

The collection float refers to how long it takes customer payments to be available for use by the company. Although the checks from customers become deposits, they may be unavailable for use because of a bank policy requiring 2 or 3 days before availability.

The Disbursement Float

The disbursement float is the period of time it takes for the deduction of vendor checks to reduce the company's cash balance at its bank. A controller who can refine his collection and disbursement floats can increase the amount of cash available perhaps by several days. By gaining access to this cash faster, the company can invest its cash and earn additional income from its investments. Table 5-2 shows how this may be accomplished.

As Table 5-2 illustrates, if a company can decrease its float time on its cash receipts by only 3 days per year, it will generate additional income of $2,952 per year, plus show an increase of cash available of $49,200. Additionally, if the controller can somehow increase its float time for cash disbursements by another 3 days per year, the company will have additional cash available of $46,800. If we obtain a yield of

Table 5-2. Projected Benefits of Optimizing "The Float"			
	Cash receipts	Cash disbursements	Total cash
Annual cash flows ($)	6,000,000	5,700,000	11,700,000
Divided by 365 days per year = cash flows per day ($)	16,400	15,600	32,000
Estimated increase in cash flows			
Increase by 1 day ($)	16,400	15,600	32,000
Increase by 2 days ($)	32,800	31,200	64,000
Increase by 3 days ($)	49,200	46,800	96,000
Estimated return on invested idle cash (assume 6% return)			
Estimated return for 1 day ($)	984	936	1,920
Estimated return for 2 days ($)	1,968	1,872	3,840
Estimated return for 3 days ($)	2,952	2,808	5,760
Overall annual benefit (cash plus est. return)			
Overall increase by 1 day ($)	17,384	16,536	33,920
Overall increase by 2 days ($)	34,768	33,072	67,840
Overall increase by 3 days ($)	52,152	49,608	101,760

6% on the additional cash, this will translate into additional income of $2,808 per year.

If the controller is able to do both (decrease the cash receipts float by 3 days, as well as increase the cash disbursements float by 3 days), an additional $96,000 of increased cash flow would be available, and that amount would increase by the assumed earnings of $5,760, for an increased overall cash flow of over $100,000 per year. Another chapter in this book describes some techniques that may accomplish just that—decrease the cash flow for receipts and increase the cash flow for disbursements.

Reducing the Collection Float

When trying to analyze the current situation and reducing the overall time for the collection float, the three items usually considered are the time the bank takes to process its collection, the time the mail is collected, and general processing time when the organization receives the checks. If all three of these processes are reviewed, along with suggestions on how to reduce the time spent on each process, the overall collection float will probably be reduced, which means that the checks are going to be received quicker. Below are some suggestions for each element of the collection float.

The Availability of Funds by the Banker

Each bank may have different policies regarding how soon the business has access to it funds. The type of deposit items as well as the location of the bank may affect the bank's policy. The controller should ascertain the bank's policy and negotiate it by comparing its terms with other local banks, checking with other local businesses to see what it has for availability, and determining the cutoff time for making daily deposits. Generally, the larger banks have more flexibility in negotiating these terms. Even if a reduction of only 1 or 2 days occurs, this is a good start to reducing the overall collection float.

Collection of Mail at the Post Office

Post office boxes receive mail continuously throughout the day. Thus, the business needs to determine the time of day when the majority of the mail appears in the post office box and make its pick-up accordingly. Another possibility is to make more than one trip per day to the post office to collect the mail. Although this suggestion may seem extreme, if the collection float reduces by just 1 day, we are one step closer to achieving our overall goal.

Other Possible Forms of Payment

The collection on some forms of payment occurs quicker. For example, wire transfers and electronic fund transfers (EFT) can reduce the collection float by another day or two. The controller should explore the option of having customers with large balances pay using either wire transfers or EFT rather than sending regular checks through the mail. Electronic data interchange (EDI) is another option the controller may wish to explore. All of these options reduce the collection float.

Lockboxes

Lockboxes are centralized locations provided primarily by a commercial bank. Customers send their payments directly to the lockbox rather than to the creditor, so the processing of payments and crediting to creditor's account occur much faster. Traditionally lockboxes reduce the collection float up to 3 days for out-of-town checks and approximately 1 day for local and regional checks. Many small businesses do not explore the opportunities that lockboxes provide because of the perception it may be too expensive. However, in some cases, lockboxes may not only reduce the collection float but may also improve the overall internal controls of a business.

In this chapter, we considered cash flow and its integral parts of collections, disbursements, and cash availability. We calculated the cash conversion cycle, and Table 5-1 illustrated its key areas. Table 5-2 displayed the process to optimize the "float."

Next, in chapter 6, we discuss many elements pertaining to the management of trade accounts receivable.

CHAPTER 6

The Management of Accounts Receivable

This chapter discusses accounts receivable management and includes a financial analysis worksheet and suggestions on establishing credit policies. This chapter also contains information regarding obtaining a security interest and guarantees, accepting P-cards from customers, and officer notes receivables. A discussion of the differences between generally accepted accounting principles (GAAP) and Internal Revenue Service (IRS) regulations regarding accounting for bad debts concludes this chapter.

The Establishment of an Effective Credit Policy

To attract new customers and increase sales volume, a company generally must extend trade credit. Although sales may increase, a potential exists for increased expenses in the form of bad debts, additional bookkeeping and accounting costs, and perhaps additional personnel costs to monitor and collect the accounts receivable. An effective credit policy must be established and enforced to control some of these additional costs, especially the potential for bad debts.

A Financial Analysis Worksheet

All controllers must understand the overall relationship of the accounts receivable function and its impact on financial statements. They should review both historical and current financial records and prepare a financial analysis worksheet. Table 6-1 illustrates some of the relevant information that may be gathered.

When reviewing the information contained in Table 6-1, the controller determines which area(s) need improvement and the potential impact

Table 6-1. Accounts Receivable Financial Analysis Worksheet					
	Year 1	Year 2	Year 3	Year 4	Year 5
Annual charge sales					
Accounts receivable outstanding at end of year					
Current					
1–30 days past due					
31–60 days past due					
61–90 days past due					
Over 90 days past due					
Total					
Days sales outstanding					
Average balance of accounts receivable/365 days divided by net credit sales					
Bad debt expense					
Relationship of the allowance for doubtful accounts and the balance of outstanding accounts receivable					
Allow for doubtful accounts/ending balance of accounts receivable					

the change(s) might have on the operating efficiency of the organization. I recommend a 5-year comparison and trend analysis, as illustrated above.

Establishing Credit Policies

Before any credit is given, a complete policy should be prepared and discussed with designated members of the management team. Credit bureaus and local organizations, including the Small Business Administration (SBA), often provide seminars on how to establish appropriate credit policies. To review existing forms available to help with the credit and collection process, local Chambers of Commerce are a good resource. The overall process and policies would normally include the credit application form, the customer review process of approved or unapproved, the verifying of information on the credit application, how the customers are notified of acceptance or rejection, and how a credit limit is established for each customer.

Additionally, the terms of the sale need to be established, such as 2/10, net 30. Review your competition in the same industry to see what they are doing.

The business should hold one of its employees accountable for the credit and collection function. Most small businesses do not assign this responsibility to the controller; however, the controller is usually better qualified than most to monitor and understand the impact slow collections and inappropriate extension of credit have on the overall profits of an organization.

Financial Ratios Pertaining to Accounts Receivable

Previous chapters of this book have suggested several relevant financial ratios applicable to accounts receivable. You may want to review those chapters again before proceeding.

A, B, & C Customers

In another chapter, we will discuss accounts payable vendors. Accounts receivable customers can have similar principles applied to them. By categorizing customers as A, B, or C, different credit limits, as well as different policies and procedures, affect each group. For example, "A" customers may account for approximately 65% of total sales volume but only consist of about 15% of total customers, "B" customers may generate about 25% of total volume and account for 25% of total customer base, while "C" customers may consist of 10% of sales volume and represent 60% of total customers. By emphasizing the major customer group (either by sales volume or by customers), the credit and collection function can focus on the largest area of potential concern.

Approval and Rejection Letters

Once the company has determined who is, and who is not, creditworthy, and establishes a credit limit for those considered creditworthy, the company notifies the customer in a professional and courteous manner. The Equal Credit Opportunity Act, and specifically Regulation B, requires a timely response whether the customer receives credit or not. If the customer does not receive credit, the notification should be in writing, outlining the reasons for the credit denial, and perhaps giving them an opportunity to reapply in the future.[1] Review thoroughly Regulation B before implementing any final credit policies and procedures.

Obtaining Additional Security on Accounts Receivable Balances

Even though a company may have the best policies and procedures set up to monitor accounts receivable performance, some customers either will extend beyond the company's credit terms or will be unable to pay the amounts within an acceptable time. When this happens, the person responsible for the credit function should seek ways to help reduce the overall risk of a customer not paying at all. In some cases, obtaining a security interest, guarantees, or both accomplishes this.

Obtaining a Security Interest

As noted previously, the intent of this action is to help reduce bad debts. The obtaining of a security interest helps to protect the creditor if the debtor is unable to pay. The Uniform Commercial Code (UCC) allows a creditor to enter into a security agreement with the debtor, and when the creditor files the form(s) with the appropriate local and state governmental agencies, it becomes public information that allows other companies to determine what security interests are in existence.[2]

Generally, two types of security interests are available in practice. One pertains to a specific obligation, such as the total balance of a customer's account, and the other pertains to specific products, such as inventory and equipment sold. Each type has its specific requirements for filing, and the controller needs to be aware of what is required and when.

Obtaining a Guarantee

A personal or corporate guarantee from the customer may be appropriate, depending on the customer. In both cases, the guarantee should be in writing, specifying interest rates and due dates. Before the final guarantee, the controller should consult the company's legal counsel.

Shortening the Receivable Cycle and the Collection Pattern

Previous chapters presented several alternatives regarding shortening the receivable cycle and increasing the collection of accounts receivable. You may want to review this information before proceeding.

Accepting P-Cards From Customers

Some companies have been using P-cards (procurement cards) for about 20 years. If a company is not accepting P-cards, it may be losing a significant amount of business. The traditional P-card replaces the usual sales invoice on a charge basis and allows customers to purchase items directly from a specific company without using purchase orders and other techniques that may slow down the process.[3] A P-card is similar to many credit cards. It allows the customer to accumulate its purchases for a specific period, and an electronic payment occurs within a couple of days. Although some initial costs are incurred (computer costs) and there is an ongoing transaction fee, it is estimated that approximately 30% of all businesses today use some sort of P-card. Two of the primary reasons the creditor uses P-cards are to eliminate practically all collection activities and to greatly expedite the cash flow process. The controller of a small business should explore how to set up and accept P-cards.

Officers' Notes Receivables

When the owner or officer of an organization borrows from the business, and whether the transaction involves cash or other assets of the organization, the controller should ensure that the owner or officer signs a promissory note specifying the amount, repayment date, and interest rate. The IRS often investigates when an amount appears on a corporation's tax return, as the amounts due from officers appear on a separate line on the corporation's tax return. The controller should explore other ways to handle this loan, such as dividends or bonuses, for example.

IRS Versus GAAP Accounting for Bad Debts

Accounting for Bad Debts According to GAAP

How an organization accounts for potential or actual bad debts depends on whether the organization is using the cash or accrual methods of reporting income. Assuming that the business is using the accrual method when recording the sale, an estimate determines how much of the receivable is uncollectible.

The estimated bad debt calculation can come from industry statistics or experience of the organization. GAAP states a better matching of revenues and expenses is realized when the sales and the corresponding estimated bad debts appear in the same period.[4]

For example, if the sales of a company for the month of June are $2,150,000 and, based on past experience, 1% of all accounts receivable are estimated to be uncollectible, the sales would be recorded in the month of June as follows:

$$\text{Accounts receivable} - \text{trade} = 2,150,000$$

$$\text{Sales} = 2,150,000$$

During the same period, in the month of June in this case, the company would make another entry recording the potential loss for estimated bad debts. The entry would be as follows:

$$\text{Bad debt expense} = 21,500$$

$$\text{Allowance for bad debts} = 21,500$$

The above amount ($21,500) is based on total sales of $2,150,000 times an estimated bad debts percentage of 1% of sales ($2,150,000 × 0.01 = $21,500).

The income statement effect of these two transactions is to increase sales by $2,150,000 and increase bad debt expense by $21,500. This translates into a net profit of $2,128,500. The impact on the balance sheet is to increase current assets (trade accounts receivable) by $2,150,000 and then create a valuation account against that account (called allowance for bad debts) for $21,500, which will create a net realizable amount from net receivables of $2,128,500 ($2,150,000 less

$21,500). This is only the first of a two-step process when complying with GAAP. The second step occurs when specific accounts are determined uncollectible. When this occurs, the account is written off the books and an entry is made as follows:

Allowance for bad debts = XXXX

Accounts receivable - trade = XXXX

For example, if we assume that a customer's account balance of $2,700 is determined to be worthless, the above entry reflects the $2,700 write-off. This entry has no impact on the income statement and does not affect net income when written off. In contrast, the net income reduction occurs when we record an estimated amount of uncollectible receivables in the same period as the recording of the sale. The impact of the actual write-off of a customer's account is the reduction of the allowance for bad debts as well as the trade accounts receivable account by the same amount. Thus, the balance sheet has no overall impact at this time. The real change on the balance sheet occurs when we record the estimated bad debts (again, in the same period as when we record the overall trade accounts receivable). We now achieve the overall matching principle (recognizing revenue and recording the estimated expenses associated with it in the same period) in accordance with GAAP.

IRS Rules Pertaining to Bad Debts

The IRS does not allow a company to take a tax deduction for any bad debts until the account receivable becomes uncollectible. Even though a company may use the accrual method according to GAAP as outlined previously, the IRS states that no amount for bad debts are deductible until the amount is determined to be worthless.[5] Thus, a permanent timing difference develops between reporting net income on the income statement and taxable income on the tax return. The IRS is not concerned about the amount estimated to be uncollectible according to GAAP, but rather requires the taxpayer to wait until the amount becomes worthless before any deduction appears on the tax return. Thus, the amount reflected as net income on the income statement and the amount of taxable income on the corporation's tax return could be significantly different.

In this chapter, we discussed the management of accounts receivable. Table 6-1 presented an example of a worksheet often used to analyze trade accounts receivable. Chapter 7 discusses inventory management and many issues pertaining to inventory.

CHAPTER 7

Management of Inventory

Many small business controllers have responsibility for supervising and monitoring the overall impact of ensuring a sufficient amount of inventory is on hand to satisfy the needs of its customers, as well as minimizing its overall carrying costs. This chapter addresses areas within the inventory management process including inventory turnover, carrying costs, reorder points, different methods of inventory valuation, the ABC approach, just-in-time inventory management, direct material and direct labor costs, and cycle counting.

The Many Aspects of Inventory Management

This chapter addresses many issues the controller considers when discharging his responsibilities regarding inventory management

Inventory Turnover

Often, the largest current asset a company shows on its balance sheet is inventory. Therefore, it is important to manage efficiently and productively the inventory function, and one of the many tools available to measure productivity is the inventory turnover. Inventory turnover is the number of times a company sells its average inventory investment each year. The actual calculation is as follows:

Cost of goods sold during the past 12 months/average inventory balance during the past 12 months

For example, if a company has total cost of sales of $14,000,000 and its average inventory value at cost is $4,000,000, the inventory turnover is 3.5 times ($14,000,000/$4,000,000). To measure how a company is doing within a specific industry and to identify ways for improvement, a comparison occurs between the company information and similar companies within the same industry, in addition to an internal comparison over a 5-year period.

Carrying Costs Associated With Inventory Levels

If a company does not appropriately manage its inventory levels, a significant hidden cost of carrying high inventory levels occurs.[1] The controller calculates the costs incurred in carrying excess inventory. If a controller has determined that current carrying costs are approximately 20% of the inventory level, he can explain and illustrate how an inventory level reduction reduces overall costs.

For example, Table 7-1 illustrates how a 10% reduction in inventory levels not only increases the overall operating profit before taxes but also, just as importantly, provides the availability of additional cash.

As shown in Table 7-1, if a company reduces estimated average annual inventory levels by 10%, or by $110,000 in this illustration, profits before taxes would increase by $22,000 ($110,000 times 20% carrying costs).

Table 7-1. Impact of Carrying Costs and Inventory Levels on Profits and Cash Flow

	Current level before inventory reduction	Revised level after inventory reduction	Difference increase (decrease)
Estimated annual revenue/sales ($)	8,000,000	8,000,000	None
Estimated gross profit percentage	32.00	32.00	None
Estimated annual net income ($)	240,000	262,000	22,000
Estimated net income as a percentage of annual revenue/sales	3.00	3.28	.28
Estimated annual inventory levels ($)	1,100,000	990,000	(110,000)
Estimated inventory turnover	4.9 times	5.5 times	.60 times
Estimated inventory carrying costs (%)	20	20	None

If the overall total impact is considered, not only would annual operating profit before taxes increase by $22,000, but operating cash of about $132,000 before taxes ($110,000 reduction in inventory levels plus a savings in carrying costs of $22,000) would also be available.

Specific Examples of Carrying Costs

At a minimum, the controller, in determining how the carrying costs interact with different inventory levels, should review the following costs.[2]

Interest Costs Incurred on Short-Term Borrowings

In many cases, the amount available on a line of credit changes with the level of inventory and, in some cases, trade accounts receivable. The credit line interest relates to a bank prime rate, and 1 or 2 points, and the amount of credit line depends on the borrowing power of the business. The interest costs on a short-term line of credit often accounts for as much as 30%–40% of total carrying costs. The reason the line of credit interest cost is included in the calculation of carrying costs is that usually the line is available and needed for short-term working capital needs, such as inventory and trade accounts receivable.

Insurance and Taxes on Inventory Levels

The amount of insurance premiums and personal property taxes paid periodically (usually annually) are often associated with inventory levels on a specific date. If inventory levels decrease, insurance and property taxes will also most likely reduce.

Storage Costs

These costs often include many of the fixed occupancy costs, such as rent, utilities, and depreciation. However, as the inventory increases, additional space is often required to store the additional inventory, and it adds additional costs beyond the usual incurred fixed amount. Conversely, as inventory reduces, storage requires less space, and some cost savings often materialize. The relevant storage costs in this type of cost savings analysis are the amounts beyond the normal fixed costs.

Inventory Handling Costs

Other costs that vary with inventory levels are shipping and receiving personnel, costs of moving the inventory from one point to another, costs of counting and taking physical inventory, and all the related payroll, payroll taxes, and applicable fringe benefits associated with personnel costs. If inventory reduces, then costs associated with this category should also reduce.

As noted previously, when the controller is conducting an analysis of possible cost reductions, he should include only the amount of inventory levels beyond the fixed amounts.

Reorder Points

All businesses that sell inventory need to have policies and procedures in place to determine at what inventory level another inventory item needs to be ordered to replace the ones sold and to ensure an adequate supply of a specific inventory item is on hand to satisfy the demands of customers. Many types of inventory management software are available that calculate relevant information such as the economic order quantity (EOQ) in addition to the reorder point, based on specific information that is imputed into the computer.[3] As the controller reviews the current company policy regarding reorder points, they should be cognizant that carrying costs outlined previously are relevant when considering the overall reorder point for specific types of inventory.

Valuation of Inventory

As stated earlier, inventory is usually the largest current asset on the balance sheet of companies who sell inventory. Although the actual physical flow of goods and the assumptions used to determine the cost of sales and ending inventory may differ, generally accepted accounting principles (GAAP) state that the primary consideration in selecting an inventory valuation method is one that clearly reflects periodic income. Most merchandising organizations select one or more of the following inventory valuations methods.[4]

Specific Identification

When an organization uses this inventory valuation method, identification occurs of each sold item as well as each item that remains in the ending inventory. Companies that have a small number of costly, easily identifiable inventory items, such as jewelry and automobiles, use this method. It is also ideal for those companies that can identify sold merchandise, because, as noted previously, it is rare that the actual cost of the goods sold matches the physical flow of the goods.

Average Cost

There are two methods used in practice, depending on whether the company is using periodic or perpetual inventory methods. A count and identification of those goods unsold occurs with the ending inventory, under the periodic inventory method. The perpetual inventory method keeps a continuous record of how much inventory is on hand; thus, the ending inventory quantity is more readily available. The weighted-average cost method occurs when a company uses a periodic inventory, while the moving average calculation occurs during the maintenance of the perpetual inventory records. Under the moving average method, a calculation of a new average unit cost occurs each time the company purchases additional inventory.

First-In, First-Out (FIFO)

The FIFO method of valuing ending inventory assumes that goods are sold in the order they are purchased. If the first goods purchased, or the amount in the beginning inventory from a previous period, are the ones sold during the period, then the ones that are in ending inventory are those that were purchased at the end of the period. Thus, the ending inventory represents the most recent purchases.

Last-In, First-Out (LIFO)

The LIFO inventory method matches the current cost of the inventory with the sales for the current period. For example, under the periodic inventory method, the amount in cost of goods sold matched against the sales revenue would be the most recent costs from the most recent purchases. The remaining inventory after deducting the cost of the most recent units sold forms the value of the ending inventory.

The LIFO Reserve

Some companies may use LIFO for tax purposes and another method for financial statement purposes. When this happens, a LIFO reserve (also called an Allowance to Reduce Inventory Levels to LIFO) appears to account for the change in the inventory levels by using two different acceptable methods. The allowance account reduces the inventory account (a contra account) on the balance sheet during the preparation of financial statements.

Lower of Cost or Market Method

One of the requirements of GAAP is that the ending inventory reflects on a balance sheet the lower of the previously acquired cost, the cost to repurchase it in the future, or the market value of the inventory on the balance sheet date. Under this method, the highest inventory value (called the ceiling) is net realizable value less expenses to sell and dispose. Additionally, the lowest value (called the floor) is the net realizable value plus the normal profit margin. The net realizable value is the estimated normal selling price of a product less the predictable costs to complete and dispose of the product.

The intent of the various inventory methods described is to help an organization accurately calculate its net income. Whether a company initially adopts FIFO or LIFO depends on company management and its overall objectives; however, once the selection of the inventory method occurs, I recommend the consistent application from period to period. If the inventory valuation method requires a change, a complete analysis should occur, outlining the pros and cons of the current and proposed inventory methods, including the impact on the overall operating profit, additional disclosures, and perhaps pro forma financial information.

Inventory Management Using the ABC Approach

As noted in previous chapters, any business that sells inventory can use the ABC approach in managing its inventory levels. The ability to categorize the inventory by different criteria, such as class, item, or geographic area, is required. Some computer software packages allow sorting of inventory products based on quantity sold. Once the small business categorizes the inventory as A, B, & C based on sales, the controller identifies the proper amount of attention to each category. For example, tight controls are common for "A" items, as this inventory group may account for 60%–75% of all sales. The inventory controls for the "B" group may be less as compared to the "A" group, but still more than the "C" group. Although the ABC approach may seem cumbersome and difficult to monitor, its intent is to identify the inventory lines that contribute most to the overall company profit and monitor them more effectively than before without the A, B, or C grouping.

Just-in-Time (JIT) Inventory

Many companies over the past years have allowed other companies to provide its inventory on an "as-needed basis." One of the major purposes of JIT inventory is to reduce the overall costs associated with inventory. JIT allows a vendor to have the exact quantity of inventory it needs, when it needs it. No longer is excess inventory sitting in the warehouse, waiting for a customer, and since the user is not storing the inventory, the elimination of many of the costs identified previously occurs because one or two primary vendors are now providing the inventory based on expected needs.[5]

Direct Material and Direct Labor Costs

Manufacturing companies differ from merchandising companies in that manufacturing companies change the final product (the inventory they purchased). When a company transforms one product into another, it incurs specific costs. Two of the primary costs incurred by a manufacturing company are direct material and direct labor. Direct materials include materials acquired that are part of its manufacturing process and traced directly to the product. Direct materials do not normally include incidental and minor items, such as supplies or indirect materials. Direct labor often includes the wages and related employee benefits that require time (labor) to alter the sold product. Although a discussion of manufacturing overhead is beyond the scope of this book, it is the third manufacturing cost normally incurred to produce inventory.

Cycle Counting, Inventory Controls, and Physical Inventory Procedures

All companies that sell inventory should take a physical count of what they currently have on hand, compare that amount with the amount recorded in the computer, and make whatever adjustments to update the computer to the actual count on hand. An important part of this process is a printout that identifies what parts were adjusted and by how much. Management should investigate the significant changes and determine the overall impact on its financial statements.

How frequently a company takes a physical inventory is based on the policy of the organization;[6] however, in my opinion, it should be taken at least twice a year. Whenever a physical count occurs, every item is part of the process. Later, through a defined process, the inventory count omits obsolete and unsaleable items, and controls set up to properly segregate and dispose of it. Rather than waiting only once a year to count the inventory, many companies have instituted a continuous count, or a cycle count.[7] Some organizations suggest that inventory counting occur daily, either before or after the normal workday. Others suggest that cycle counting be accomplished on a regular basis, but not daily.

Regardless of management's philosophy regarding cycle counting, the ABC approach mentioned previously can also apply. For example, A items, which may account for 60%–70% of a company's sales, may be counted 4 to 6 times per year, whereas B items, which account for perhaps 10%–15% of the sales volume, may be counted only 2 to 3 times per year. Lastly, C items may be counted only once or twice per year, as they account for a much smaller sales volume.

Cycle counting is different in that only experienced inventory personnel are part of this process. Normally when a physical inventory occurs once a year, all employees are required to help with the process. By using only qualified personnel to perform cycle counting, they are familiar with the inventory items and often perform a much more credible job.

In this chapter, we discussed the management of inventory, including inventory turnover, carrying costs, reorder points, and different methods of inventory valuation. We also discussed JIT inventory as well as cycle counting, direct materials, and direct labor. Table 7-1 illustrated how carrying costs and inventory levels impacts cash and profits.

The next chapter discusses short-term financial planning, including working capital, management of accounts payable, and commitment letters, just to name a few items.

CHAPTER 8

Short-Term Financial Planning

As noted previously, a company can have profitable operations and still be unable to pay its obligations in a timely manner. A major change in the working capital items (current assets and current liabilities) of the business may create this situation. This chapter focuses on short-term financial planning, including managing accounts payable vendors; different types of company commitment agreements, including certificates of insurance, sales and use tax exemption certificates; volume purchase guarantees; the Uniform Commercial Code (UCC) and security agreements; and inventory returns and restocking charges.

The Need for Additional Working Capital

As a company grows and increases its sales volume, chances are the balances in accounts receivable, inventory, and accounts payable increases. Even though inventory is increasing, vendors providing trade credit still expect payment on time or within the discount period, if applicable. Controllers need to be aware of the impact accounts receivable, inventory, and accounts payable have on the short-term financial health of a company. A continuous monitoring occurs within all three of these categories. A discussion follows regarding some of the important aspects pertaining to accounts payable.

Managing Accounts Payable

For many small businesses, one of the primary sources of short-term financing is trade credit from vendors. When a company is monitoring cash management, a review of the relationship with vendors and the availability of discounts should occur on a regular basis.

To help a new controller understand the relationship between the purchases and the accounts payable functions, a financial analysis is prepared to obtain key relationships and ratios. Table 8-1 contains a suggested format to analyze purchasing and accounts payable performance over a 5-year period. This type of analysis may also prove informative for controllers who are not new to the organization but want to get a better understanding of what is happening in the accounts payable and purchase relationship.

Table 8-1. *Accounts Payable Financial Analysis Worksheet for Years Ended December 31, 2003, Through 2008*

Various general ledger and financial statement information	2003	2004	2005	2006	2007	2008
Sales in dollars						
Purchases in dollars						
Cost of goods sold percentage						
Accounts payable at end of year						
Purchase discounts available						
Purchase discounts taken						
Calculation of various trends and ratios						
1. Accounts payable to sales ratio	(Accounts payable/net sales) × 100. **Example:** Accounts payable balance as of 12/31/03 is $1,200,000. Net sales for the year 2003 are $7,350,000. Ratio calculated as follows: (1,200,000/7,350,000) × 100 = 16.3%. This means that 16.3% of the company's sales are being funded by its suppliers.					
2. Average payment period	Accounts payable/(purchases/360). This indicates how quickly accounts payable is being paid.					
3. Percentage of purchase discounts taken	Purchase discounts taken/purchase discounts available. This displays the percentage of purchase discounts available versus those that were taken. This can be a good monitoring device to take advantage of all available discounts.					

A, B, & C Vendors

Both the inventory of a business and accounts payable vendors are categorized into A, B, & C classifications. A company communicates with its vendors to monitor the quality of service received and to resolve expeditiously any problems. The controller may effectively utilize an approach similar to a previous discussion, where each vendor is either A, B, or C.

"A" Vendors

These are the suppliers, usually only a few, who account for approximately 80% of all inventory purchases. The inventory items purchased from "A" vendors usually have the fastest turnover rate, thus it is important that sufficient quantities be on hand. Because these inventory items, and the vendors who provide them, account for the bulk of the sales, the communication process should take place on a regular recurring basis. The controller should review the contract terms with "A" vendors at least semiannually and more often if the need arises.

"B" Vendors

These vendors usually provide approximately 10%–15% of the inventory, and the items are less critical than those obtained from "A" vendors. However, the communication process should still be quite active. Nothing less than annual review of "B" vendor contracts should occur.

"C" Vendors

Although these vendors are more numerous than "A" and "B" vendors, they usually account for a very small percentage (5%–10%) of the total purchases. The communication process usually occurs when needed or when problems arise.

Different Types of Company Commitment Agreements

Because of the business expertise controllers possess, they need to be involved in agreements signed by the organization. Some of the agreements may require disclosures as part of the external financial statements or, just as importantly, the agreements may also require the organization to perform in some way or affect the agreements with other major creditors and vendors.

Some of the more common agreements follow.

Certificate of Insurance

Usually major vendors require evidence of the amount and type of insurance coverage carried by the small business. In some cases, the vendor may ask to be an "additional insured" on the policy. Avoid this request whenever possible because it often requires additional insurance coverage that translates into additional exposure, as well as additional insurance premiums. Currently, the business's insurance carrier can provide the requested necessary information to a vendor on Form 25-S.[1]

Uniform Sales and Use Tax Exemption Certificate

Each seller and purchaser of merchandise must comply with individual state requirements regarding the collection, or exemption from collection, of sales and use taxes. The vendor must collect the tax for the state in which they deliver the inventory, if there is no exemption certificate provided. A common reason for the exemption from paying sales and use taxes includes using the inventory for wholesale, resale, or components for producing a new resold product. The requirements in each state are different, and the controller should review each jurisdiction.[2] Based on my experience, this is one area in which most states are quite active and currently exploring to raise the additional revenue needed to balance its budget.

Volume Purchase Guarantees

When dealing with one or two major vendors for the purchase of a major portion of its inventory, an agreement may be required specifying a minimum volume over a specific period to justify the price concessions and other terms. The controller should ascertain over what period of time (monthly, quarterly, etc.) it encompasses, monitor it, and review what penalties or other fees, if any, may arise because of nonperformance. As noted previously, in some cases the purchase guarantees may require disclosures as part of the external financial statements.

Uniform Commercial Code (UCC) Security Agreements

An agreement of this type establishes a secured interest in some type of personal property (meaning inventory in this case). Usually with no secured interest, the vendor has only the borrower's oral promise to pay for the inventory; however, with this type of security agreement, the business is giving an interest in the inventory to the vendor until the inventory is paid. Currently, Form UCC-1 perfects this secured interest, and the county and state where the inventory is located determines the filing of the forms.[3] The controller should contact the organization's legal advisor when any organization requests secured interests and before any are given.

Inventory Returns and Restocking Charges

Occasionally, businesses may experience slow moving or obsolete inventory items. Some vendors have very specific policies regarding allowing a customer to return merchandise and receive a credit. Other times the customer may have to negotiate the terms, the restocking charge, or both. In some cases, the restocking charge can be 10%–15% of the inventory value returned for credit.[4] The controller should be familiar with the agreement terms and ascertain if it is advantageous to return merchandise to the vendor, in spite of the restocking or any other charges.

This chapter discussed short-term financial planning, including the need for additional working capital. It also discussed security agreements and guarantees, as well as commitment agreements and certificates of insurance. Table 8-1 illustrated the analysis of accounts payable over an extended period.

Chapter 9 changes to a discussion of property, plant, and equipment, and includes the role of the small business controller in capital investment decisions.

CHAPTER 9

Property, Plant, and Equipment

When an organization invests a large sum in property, plant, and equipment, if a mistake occurs in selecting which projects to approve, the effects can be significant and transparent for many periods. The long lives of fixed assets, plus the multitude of techniques that a controller uses to evaluate whether to invest the funds in a specific project, can have profound and lingering effects on future profits and cash flows.

This chapter discusses the role of the small business controller in capital investment decisions and reviews several methods used in practice to evaluate capital investment projects, including the payback, net present value (NPV), and internal rate of return methods.

The Role of the Controller in Capital Investment Decisions

Although the role of the controller in a small business will vary regarding the process used to acquire fixed assets, someone within the organization, usually the controller, should have the ability and expertise to conduct a careful analysis of the investment opportunities, ensuring the best possible utilization of the funds. They participate in the process by evaluating the capital investment proposals, as well as determining how to structure or finance the project. In some small businesses, the controller is also involved in the preparation of an annual capital expenditure budget that often includes requests from departmental managers or other management personnel. Some of the more common categories for capital requests are major repairs and maintenance, improvements to current building structures, or additions to fixed assets (e.g., new equipment).

Capital Investment Evaluation Methods

The evaluation of capital investment projects often includes several methods. Some of the methods described have specific limitations, while others measure specific key areas, such as how quickly the investment returns. A capital investment process should be in place to determine, based on previously established specific criteria, which projects are accepted or rejected. As noted previously, even though the role of the controller in the evaluation of specific projects varies from company to company, a common role the controller provides is a cost-benefit analysis determining if the project fits within the financial framework identified by the organization. Below are listed some common methods used by many small businesses to evaluate potential investment alternatives.

Payback Method

This method is one of the easiest to use and focuses on how much time it takes to recapture the initial investment. The payback method measures how long it takes in future cash flows to recover its original investment.[1] For example, if the business has a possible investment costing $35,000, and based on its projections of future profits after taxes of $5,000 per year over the next 7 years, the information reflects a conversion to cash flows rather than profits to measure how long it takes to recapture its original investment.

The calculation is as follows:

Future projected net profit after taxes per year = $5,000

Add depreciation per year ($35,000/7 years) = $5,000

Estimated annual cash provided from operations = $10,000

Estimated payback period
($35,000/$10,000) = 3.5 years

The future projected net profit after taxes has to be converted to estimated cash flow per year because the payback method uses annual cash inflows rather than annual net income. The advantage to this method is that it is easy to understand and calculate. Under this method, the projects that contain the shorter payback period usually rank higher than those with longer periods. The logic is that by getting the original investment returned faster, it becomes liquid and thus less risky. The investment has less of a chance for long-term interest rates and general economic conditions to affect it. The major disadvantage of this method is that it does not consider the time value of money. If the payback period extends beyond 1 year, the calculation of an interest rate factor into the time value of a dollar received today versus in 3.5 years is important, as in the previous illustration. This is a good method to use as a starting point, but other calculations should occur as well.

Discounted Cash Flow Models

By its nature, capital investment projects usually extend beyond 1 year and some consideration occurs for the value of a dollar today versus a dollar received some time in the future. The various discounted cash flow models discussed below consider the time value of money.

Net Present Value (NPV) Method

One of the more popular methods considering the time value of money is the NPV method. It factors into calculating the present value of the estimated cash inflows using a predetermined discount rate. For example, if we use the same information per the previous illustration and use a different valuation method, we arrive at a different conclusion.

An expected investment in the capital project is $35,000, the estimated future cash inflows per year after depreciation and taxes is $10,000 for the next 7 years, and the company has determined that the investment must produce future cash flows after taxes of 12% to improve the overall financial position of the organization. With this information, the NPV calculation is as follows:

Cost of investment (now year 0) = $35,000

Estimated annual cash inflows for years 1–7

($10,000) × 12% discount factor

(7 years @ 12%) = 4.56376 using the table of the present value of an
ordinary annuity of 1 = 45,638

Estimated NPV = $10,638

Based on the above calculation, the NPV is a positive $10,638, which
indicates that the overall return to the organization is greater than 12%.
The overall value of the business will increase, and the investment is
acceptable based on the criteria established.

As stated previously, one of the advantages to using the NPV method is
the consideration of the time value of money. One of the subjective areas in
this calculation is the determination of the interest rate or discount factor.

Internal Rate of Return (IRR) Method

The IRR method also considers the time value of money; however, this
method finds an interest rate that equalizes the cash inflows and cash out-
flows. Although we commonly use financial calculators to compute the
exact interest rate in practice, interpolations (trial and error) can occur
for some calculations. For example, if we use the same capital investment
opportunity as outlined previously, we can calculate the IRR. In the previous example for the NPV calculation, the NPV is $10,638, assuming
a 12% cost of capital. With a positive NPV, the rate of return must be
greater than 12%.

The IRR is as follows:

Cost of investment (now – year 0) = $35,000

If we assume the interest rate might be close to 15%, estimated annual
cash inflows for years

$10,000 × 15% discount factor (7 years @ 15%) = 4.16042 using the
table of the present value of an ordinary annuity of 1 = 41,604

Estimated NPV $6,604

With this revised information, we determine that the actual return must be greater than 15%, because the NPV is still positive. By interpolation, the internal rate of return is still higher than 15% and could be approximately 20%. A similar analysis can be prepared to determine the cash break-even point.

Once the internal rate of return has been calculated (in this case estimated to be 20%), management must decide if the rate is sufficient and in line with company expectations. A common practice is to calculate the hurdle rate, discussed in another chapter of this book, compare the IRR with the hurdle rate, and as long as the IRR exceeds the hurdle rate, management usually accepts the investment proposal. One of the primary advantages of using the IRR method is that the actual return is calculated based on various assumptions and management can determine if the return is sufficient for the overall benefit of the organization.

I recommend using both the NPV and the IRR methods when reviewing capital investment proposals.

In this chapter, we presented a discussion of the acquisition of property, plant, and equipment, along with different valuation methods to determine the feasibility of the investment decision. We discussed the role of the controller in capital investment decisions, as well as the payback method, NPV method, and internal rate of return methods used in practice to arrive at an investment decision.

The next chapter discusses key points to consider when receiving capital and planning the capital structure of the small business.

CHAPTER 10

Raising Capital and the Capital Structure

Throughout this book, we discuss different types of financing. In this chapter, we examine issues including the cost of capital and costs associated with debt, equity, and retained earnings with illustrative tables to review the overall capital structure. Also presented are financial leverage, hurdle rates, and treasury stock. The chapter ends with a discussion regarding financial analysis.

Cost of Capital

Every business, public or nonpublic, large or small, will eventually need some sort of capital (funds). This funding may be required to finance working capital, long-term equipment acquisitions, or other purposes. The effective utilization of all business investments must occur, and one way of measuring such utilization is a comparison of the return on invested capital with the cost of capital. Businesses finance their operations through one (or more) of the following three sources: (a) issuing equity (stocks), (b) issuing debt (e.g., borrowing from a bank), and (c) reinvesting prior retained earnings (called financing from within). Both lenders and equity interests (shareholders) expect to earn a return on their invested funds. A comparison is made of these three investment alternatives with the calculation of the overall weighted-average cost of capital. For an investment to be worthwhile and beneficial, the return on capital must be greater than the cost of capital.

Cost of Debt

Most debt contains an interest rate and payments. Because interest expense is usually tax deductible, the net cost of the debt is the interest expense less the tax savings, as follows:

Cost of debt = the interest expense × (100% – the effective tax rate of the business)

Cost of Equity

Unlike debt, which usually requires both interest and principal payments over a specific period, equity usually does not have a set amount the company must pay; however, equity financing still has costs associated with it. Even though the company is nonpublic, the common shareholders still expect to receive, although not necessarily in the form of cash payments, a specific return on their equity investments to maintain an acceptable share price. When this cost of equity capital is calculated, an adjustment occurs for specific risk factors, thus increasing or decreasing the overall cost of equity capital based on investor subjective analysis.

Therefore, the true cost of equity capital is the rate of return required by the common shareholders. The capital asset pricing model (CAPM) is a good vehicle to use to calculate this expected return on equity financing.

Cost of Retained Earnings

Investors generally expect retained earnings to produce a rate of return that is comparable to dividends received from dividend-paying stocks. The CAPM referred to above is also appropriate for the determination of costs associated with retained earnings financing.

The Overall Capital Structure

It is usually cheaper to issue debt than equity because of the tax advantages associated with interest. However, depending on interest rate fluctuations and debt amount, the cost for debt may be considerably higher than equity financing because of the potential risks associated with default, thus affecting the company's overall interest rates. The overall cost of capital and calculation to determine the optimal mix of financing that minimizes the cost of capital and increases the overall value to the business must be determined.

Table 10-1 highlights some key items to consider when deciding between debt and equity financing alternatives.

The following is an example of the cost of capital calculation:

Assumptions:

1. $600,000 of debt outstanding for a full year with an interest rate of 8%
2. Corporate tax rate of 30%

a. Calculation of cost of debt

Interest expense × (1 − tax rate)/amount of debt

$48,000 (interest expense = $600,000 × 0.08 for 1 year)

.70(100 − 30% tax rate)/$600,000(total amount of debt outstanding) = 5.6% cost of debt ($48,000 × .70 = $33,600 $33,600/$600,000 = **5.6%**)

Author's note: Use caution when determining if the principal amount of the loan is calculated based on the interest method (where the full amount of the principal is loaned as illustrated above) or the discount method (where only the net proceeds of the loan are received). The net amount received will affect the above calculations.

Table 10-1. Comparison of Debt Versus Equity Financing	
Debt	**Equity**
Regular interest payments are usually required, and cash needs to be generated to repay principal and interest.	Usually no payments are required.
Creditors usually require some sort of collateral to secure the debt.	No collateral is required by equity investors.
Interest payments are usually tax deductible.	Payments given to equity investors (called dividends) are not tax deductible.
Although the issuance of debt may not affect the overall control of the organization, certain restrictive covenants may appear.	By issuing additional shares of equity, the control of the organization may be diluted.

Calculation of Cost of Equity

The following calculation determines the cost of equity:

Risk-free return + beta (average stock return – risk-free return).

As noted previously, one method used to calculate the cost of equity capital is the CAPM. This model determines the risk of holding equity shares of a specific company as compared to the risk of holding a mix of stocks offered in the open market.[1] To understand how nonpublic companies use this model, I define certain terminology below.

The "risk" referred to above consists of three elements. The first element is the rate of return an investor could get from a risk-free investment, usually defined as a security guaranteed by the U.S. government. Second is the possible return from an average risk security. Last is a company's beta, which is the amount a company's stock returns differ from the average-risk stocks. For example, a beta of 1.0 would mean that a specific stock is exactly equal in risk as compared to the average stock, while a beta of 0.70 would indicate lower risk and a beta of 1.2 would indicate higher risk. Below is an example showing a calculation for the cost of equity capital:

Assumptions:

1. The risk-free cost of capital is 4%.
2. The average return based on Standards and Poor's 500 Index is 9%.
3. The nonpublic company's beta is 1.8.

With this information, the calculation for cost of equity capital is as follows:

4.0% + (1.8 × [9.0% – 4.0%]) = **13.0% cost of equity capital**

Although assumptions may vary, the previous illustration demonstrates that most nonpublic companies will usually have a high beta because of its risks and lack of marketability. Thus, nonpublic common stock is usually the most expensive type of financing.

The weighted-average cost of capital comes after the cost of capital for both debt and equity.[2] Table 10-2 shows the calculation.

Table 10-2. Calculation of Weighted-Average Cost of Capital			
Assumptions			
Debt			
1. Amount of interest-bearing debt oustanding for entire year	$600,000		
2. Interest rate (as stated previously)	8%		
3. Income tax rate (as stated previously)	30%		
4. Average cost of debt capital (as stated previously)	5.6%		
Equity			
5. Amount of common stock outstanding for entire year	$1,200,000		
6. Average cost of equity capital (as stated previously)	13.00%		
Type of funding	**Amount of funding ($)**	**Percentage cost (%)**	**Dollar cost ($)**
Debt	600,000	5.6	33,600
Equity	1,200,000	13.0	156,000
Totals	1,800,000	10.53	189,600
Based on the above calculations and assumptions, the weighted-average cost of capital is **10.53%**.			

Financial Leverage

Financial leverage is using debt to increase the overall return on equity and uses the ratio of debt to equity. This relationship of debt to total stockholders' equity, often referred to as the debt to equity ratio, debt ratio, financial leverage ratio, or leverage ratio, measures the extent an organization relies on its debt financing.

Some analysts state the maximum the debt to equity ratio should be is 2 to 1, with up to one-third of the total debt in the long-term category, depending on the industry in which the company operates. A high ratio may indicate potential difficulty in paying the debt and obtaining more funding.[3] If a business can obtain a rate of return on the common stockholders' equity greater than the interest rate paid for the debt, the leverage will increase the earnings per share and the value of the stock. However, if the reverse is true, the value of highly leveraged stock will decrease the same two items. The calculation is as follows:

All liabilities (short-term and long-term)/total stockholders' equity

Hurdle Rates

Hurdle rates are the rates (or amounts) that the returns exceed the company weighted-average cost of capital. Previously, the weighted-average cost of capital was calculated, and to put the hurdle rate in perspective, the hurdle rate must exceed the cost of capital or the overall value of the firm will decrease. The use of the hurdle rate differs from company to company. For example, some large companies, with many divisions, may have different hurdle rates for different divisions, indicating different risks. Additionally, if the calculation of the weighted-average cost of capital were 12%, an organization would want to earn at least 12% (after taxes) on its capital investments and expenditures to increase the value of its stockholders' equity.[4]

Treasury Stock

Treasury stock is reacquired stock of a company. It is not outstanding stock when calculating earnings per share or dividends and has no voting privileges. The balance sheet shows treasury stock as a reduction of stockholders' equity, and when the company buys back its own stock (called treasury stock) the overall impact on the financial statements is a reduction of cash and a reduction of stockholders' equity (by creating a treasury stock account). Companies buy back their shares for several reasons, which might include management feeling the stock is undervalued. Another reason is to allow the shareholders an opportunity to get cash out of the corporation, without any dividend distribution. Additional reasons may be to give to employees as bonuses and additional compensation or to put the shares into an employee stock ownership plan. The favorable capital gains treatment currently offered by the Internal Revenue Service code allows the shareholders to keep a greater portion of the proceeds.

Buying back shares increases the earnings per share calculation, as the denominator of the calculation reduces by decreasing the shares outstanding.

Financial Analysis

For many years, Robert Morris Associates (RMA) provided various services to bankers, which included the calculation of many ratios and trends to highlight specific financial areas. In July 2000, Robert Morris Associates changed its name to Risk Management Association, still known as RMA, but expanding its services.[5] My experience with many banking institutions that use reports from RMA has been very positive, and in many cases, the banker shares major portions of the RMA reports with the business controller. This is very relevant information as it displays what information the banker is reviewing, in addition to what concerns may arise when negotiating a renewal of the existing line of credit.

Once a review of the report occurs, and even if a banker shares only part, the controller needs to be proactive. For example, when the business line of credit was renewed last year, did the banker express concerns about the reduction in inventory turnover or the large amount of past-due receivables? If so, the controller could focus on these items and resolve the issues. Even if a significant change in the financial statements cannot happen within a year, I strongly recommend the controller write a letter to the banker that accompanies the year-end financial statements (or the interim financial statements if applicable) to explain both the positive and other trends. The controller should address in a professional and meaningful way what is happening to make progress in those areas. By being proactive, the controller sends a message that he is aware of what is happening within the organization and that steps are mitigating or improving the current situation. Experience suggests that this type message will be much more meaningful to a banker and other major creditors than not sharing any plans or results at all or merely reacting to a situation when it develops. The controller needs to highlight trends and provide additional information to outside stakeholders who do not have access to the day-to-day happenings in the organization.

As noted previously, ratio analysis is very important, and the controller must understand what ratios the banker emphasizes. For example, if the banker is concerned about liquidity and the ability of the business to repay its obligations on a timely basis, he or she might emphasize the current ratio (current assets divided by current liabilities). Because the controller knows what items make up both categories, he can manage the results and emphasize in a periodic report to the banker what is happening to alter the ratio and make it more in line with expectations. Although one of the primary reasons for this communication is to maintain banking support, the internal management must be aware of the banker's concerns and address specifically the plans to resolve those concerns.

This chapter discussed key points when raising capital and planning the capital structure. We calculated the cost of debt, equity, and retained earnings. Additionally, we calculated the weighted-average cost of capital. Tables 10-1 and 10-2 illustrated some of the key areas in the chapter.

The next chapter discusses budgets and planning, and presents several tables to show how the reports are prepared.

CHAPTER 11

Planning and Budgeting

A company cannot survive long without some sort of planning and budgeting. In this chapter, we discuss the annual planning and budget process, including the break-even point, the margin of safety, and free cash flow. Additionally, we present flexible budgets versus static budgets, with specific examples and illustrations. Lastly, we discuss operating and financing leases as a means to raise capital.

The Role of the Controller in Planning and Budgeting

A controller spends a significant amount of time in preparing, altering, and finalizing the annual budget. Although a discussion of the pros and cons of successful budgeting is not part of this book, it is important that small business controllers assume a leadership role in the process. The budget information is usually accumulated from many different departments and sources, and it needs one person who has the skills and expertise (such as the controller) to be responsible for putting all the information together and producing an overall companywide budget. Depending on the size and complexity of the organization, many different types of budgets are prepared and compared periodically with actual results.

The Break-Even Point

Every business needs to know its break-even point, which is the sales volume where no profit or loss occurs. It is the point where all costs and expenses equal sales.

Most accounting systems usually do not automatically generate the break-even point; however, the controller, as well as other management personnel, needs to understand how the break-even point is calculated and how it changes as various elements change.

Fixed costs are costs that do not change over a specific relevant range. Examples include such costs as real estate taxes, rental of office space, and executive salaries. Variable costs are costs that change in direct proportion to the changes in sales volume, and examples include cost of merchandise to sell, supplies, labor, and commissions.

The starting point for the break-even calculation is categorizing all expenses as fixed or variable. After this categorizing occurs, the fixed costs divided by the gross profit percentage equals the sales volume necessary to cover the fixed expenses. For example, if the business has determined that its annual gross profit is 30% and its annual fixed expenses are $1,200,000, the annual sales necessary to break even are $ 4,000,000 ($1,200,000/0.30). A review of all numbers (gross profit percentage, fixed costs, and variable costs) should happen at least every 6 months and should be communicated to management, especially when periodic financial statements are prepared and discussed. An organization generally is not in business to break even; however, once determined, a company can project an adequate profit using the break-even calculation as a start.

For example, using the previous figures of gross profit of 30% and fixed costs of $1,200,000, and assuming the company desires a profit before taxes of $75,000, how much sales are necessary to generate the desired level of profit? The calculation involves dividing the desired profits ($75,000 in this case) by the gross profit percentage (30%). This amount is $250,000. In other words, to generate an annual profit of $75,000 before taxes, with a gross profit rate of 30% and fixed costs of $1,200,000, a company must produce annual sales of $4,250,000. The annual break-even sales have increased from $4,000,000 previously to a revised sales level of $4,250,000 because of the desired level of profits.

The break-even point has three possible changes: it can change the level of fixed expenses, the amount of variable costs, or the selling price of the products. Management needs to know how overall profits and the break-even point change as any of the three elements change.

Margin of Safety

Once the controller and other management employees know how to calculate the break-even point and how it changes, the margin of safety, defined as the amount of sales volume over and above the break-even point, becomes relevant. If a company is enjoying profitable operations, the margin of safety also indicates the amount by which sales can decline before the company reaches its break-even point. The calculation is as follows:

Current sales level – break-even point/current sales level.

Another way to calculate this is by comparing current level of sales with the projected break-even point. By subtracting the current level of sales (assuming a profit) from the break-even sales, the margin of safety appears. The larger the company's margin of safety, the less likely it will have an operating loss, which occurs when it operates below the break-even point. A smaller margin of safety indicates more risk.

Free Cash Flow

Another financial measure used to evaluate a company's operating results is free cash flow. Although the amount considered adequate varies from industry to industry, this calculation spots trends within the company rather than comparing it to other companies within a similar industry. The calculation is as follows:

Cash flow from operating activities (found on the statement of cash flows) – additions to property, plant, and equipment[1]

In practice, the deduction of other unusual items occurs to help understand the true significance of this amount.

Fixed Expenses and Costs Coverage Ratio

Another ratio calculated is the fixed expenses and other fixed payments as compared to cash flow from operations. The calculation is as follows:

Fixed expenses + fixed payments/cash flows from operations

This ratio provides an analysis of how cash flow covers fixed expenses and other fixed payments and indicates how much cash is currently required, as well as future problems if sales decline.

The controller should have a good working knowledge as to how the ratios are interrelated and be aware that sometimes concentrating on one set of ratios can cause an effect on other ratios. For example, if the controller is concerned about the current ratio (current assets divided by current liabilities) and tries to improve it by borrowing money on a long-term basis but not spending the cash, even though the current ratio may improve, another ratio, the ratio of long-term debt to stockholders' equity, is negatively affected.

Using Flexible Budgets Instead of Static Budgets

A static budget is prepared for only one level of activity. If a company is 100% certain that it will achieve a specific level of activity during the coming year, static budgets are appropriate. However, most companies are not very certain and use flexible budgets. A flexible budget allows for changes in sales volume as well as changes in variable and fixed costs. It is very similar to the traditional static budget, but allows the manager the flexibility to prepare the budget using any level of activity (sales volume). To utilize properly flexible budgets, the controller must determine how revenue and the various expense elements interact. For example, Table 11-1 shows how the flexible budget may be prepared.

Once the overall results have been finalized and a comparison of budgeted to actual performance has been made, the flexible budget is used to determine how efficient (flexible budget variance) and how effective (sales-activity variance) the overall organization has been. The efficiency is a measurement of how well the business used its inputs to produce a certain level of outputs, and effectiveness relates to the achievement of the overall sales target, in this case 27,000 units. Table 11-2 shows some sample calculations.

For example, if we use the information contained in Table 11-2, the flexible budget variance (also called the efficiency variance) would be $11,800 unfavorable. Based on the flexible budget of 25,000 units, and comparing the actual results with the budgeted amounts for the same level of activity, the efficiency variance is $11,800 unfavorable, consisting of $9,800 increased variable costs and $2,000 increased fixed costs. This is column 2 of Table 11-1, which is the difference between column

Table 11-1. Flexible Budget Illustration

	Flexible budget formula per unit	Estimated levels of activity for the year			
Units		25,000	30,000	35,000	40,000
Sales ($)	45.00	1,125,000	1,350,000	1,575,000	1,800,000
Variable costs					
Manufacturing costs ($)	20.00	500,000	600,000	700,000	800,000
Shipping and selling costs ($)	1.15	28,750	34,500	40,250	46,000
General and administrative costs ($)	0.35	8,750	10,500	12,250	14,000
Total variable costs ($)	21.50	537,500	645,000	752,500	860,000
Contribution margin (gross margin) ($)	23.50	587,500	705,000	822,500	940,000
Fixed costs					
Manufacturing costs ($)	200,000	200,000	200,000	200,000	200,000
Selling costs ($)	195,000	195,000	195,000	195,000	195,000
General and administrative costs ($)	245,000	245,000	245,000	245,000	245,000
Total fixed costs ($)	640,000	640,000	640,000	640,000	640,000
Operating income (loss) ($)		(52,500)	65,000	182,500	300,000

Table 11-2. Flexible Budget Analysis

	1 Actual results at actual activity level	2 Flexible budget variance	3 Flexible budget for actual sales activity	4 Sales volume variance	5 Static budget
Units	25,000	0	25,000	2,000 UN	27,000
Sales (in dollars)	1,125,000	0	1,125,000	90,000 UN	1,215,000
Variable costs (in dollars)	547,300	9,800 UN	537,500	43,000 F	580,500
Gross profit (contribution margin, in dollars)	577,700	9,800 UN	587,500	47,000 UN	634,500
Fixed costs (in dollars)	642,000	2,000 UN	640,000	0	640,000
Operating income (loss, in dollars)	(64,300)	11,800 UN	(52,500)	47,000 UN	(5,500)

Note: F = favorable; Un = Unfavorable.

1 and column 3. This type of variance holds someone accountable for the overall changes from budget to actual results, and in many cases, the operating managers are in the best position to explain the discrepancies.

The other variance, called the sales volume variance (also known as the effectiveness variance or the activity level variances) determines the overall objective, in this case the master budget (also called the static budget) of 27,000 units sold. Column 4 shows a total unfavorable variance of $47,000 because of the lack of sales volume (in this case, 2,000 units), which translates into lack of overall profit. Notice the fixed costs did not change within this relevant range (column 4); thus, the lack of sales volume totally accounts for the entire lack of profit of $47,000. In many cases, the sales or marketing manager is accountable for the overall difference in sales volume.

Lease Versus Debt Financing

Once an organization decides to invest scarce resources into an investment project, how will the small business pay for it? Is it a leased project and classified as an operating or capital lease, or is the project financed with a lending institution? Many small businesses choose to lease versus buying an asset for many reasons, which include a desire to keep the leased asset and corresponding liability off its balance sheet, an effort to conserve cash, and a desire to not own the equipment and return it to the lessor at the expiration of the lease agreement.

A small business controller reviews the many alternatives available and is aware of current GAAP that pertain to leasing a tangible asset.[2] Two options are currently available pertaining to leases—one is an operating lease and the other a capital lease. According to GAAP, if a lease is noncancelable and contains any one of the following four criteria, it is determined to be a capital lease:

1. The lease transfers ownership of the property to the lessee.
2. A bargain purchase option is contained in the lease. This is evident when the purchase option contained in the lease is significantly below the fair market value of the asset upon the expiration of the lease agreement, and the exercise of the option to purchase the asset is reasonably assured.

3. The lease term is equal to 75% or more of the estimated economic life of the asset leased. The controller needs to determine the economic life of the asset and I recommend using the tables that list various assets and useful lives published by the IRS. For example, if a vehicle is considered to be a 5-year property by the IRS, the controller can use that period (5 years in this case) as the estimated economic life of the asset and then compare the lease period with the 5 years to see if the 75% rule becomes relevant.

4. The minimum lease payments to the lessor equal or exceed 90% of the fair market value of the leased asset. Deduct any executory costs from the calculation to apply the 90% rule, if they are included in the normal monthly payments to the lessor.

As noted previously, if any one of the four items is contained in the lease agreement, the lessee is required to record the asset as a capital lease. This means that the lessee must reflect the asset and liability value on the face of the balance sheet. However, if the lease is not a capital lease based on the previous criteria, the asset and corresponding liability does not appear on the balance sheet but rather is as an operating lease, and rent expense appears on the income statement on a periodic basis.

Once all of the relevant information has been gathered pertaining to a possible leasing transaction versus the actual purchase of the asset, an analysis is generated by the controller to consider all aspects of the transaction.

Section 162 of the IRS Tax Code

The IRS tax code specifically addresses capital leases and operating leases and refers to Financial Accounting Standards Board (FASB) No. 13 for the treatment of leases considered capital leases.[3] Additionally, the code refers to special treatment of the lease payments that might appear on Schedule M-1 of a corporate tax return. The code also states that the facts and circumstances of each lease transaction determine if it is a capital or operating lease for tax purposes. The controller should review current literature for specific guidance.

In this chapter, we discussed the role of planning and budgeting in a small business, as well as calculating the break-even point, the margin of safety, free cash flow, and the fixed expenses and cost coverage ratio. We discussed static and flexible budgets, and Tables 11-1 and 11-2 illustrated how flexible budgets are used in practice.

Chapter 12 discusses internal sources of financing, such as reducing inventory levels, increasing accounts receivable collections, and funding from shareholders, family members, and friends.

CHAPTER 12

Obtaining Financing and Increasing Cash Flow

In this chapter, we present information regarding obtaining financing and additional ways to increase cash flow. We discuss several internal sources of financing for a company, including reduction of inventory levels, profits, increasing accounts receivable collections, and reviewing accounts payable disbursement policies. Lastly, personal funding from shareholders, family, and friends; external sources of financing, including lending institutions, factoring of accounts receivable, leasing, venture capitalists, and angel investors; and how to calculate the true cost associated with a line of credit are discussed. Several tables display the type of information and calculations involved.

As noted in other chapters of this book, even a very profitable company can incur cash flow shortages. The cash shortage may be for a short period, perhaps because of seasonal fluctuations (cycles) within the business, or may be more long term because of capital expansion plans. The controller constantly monitors the financial affairs of a business and is able to anticipate the financing need of a small business. He or she needs to be proactive in projecting when and how much financing will be needed well in advance of the actual need. With all the daily monitoring a controller needs to do, I recommend a sheet outlining the current and past trends of financing activities. Although the format and information may vary, I recommend a sheet similar to Table 12-1.

Internal Sources of Financing[1]

One of the best ways to obtain additional financing is from internal operations of a business. When starting this process, the controller reviews the way the business operates and unlocks some of its internal sources to

Table 12-1. Recap of Financing Activities Worksheet for Years Ended December 31, 2004, Through 2008

	2004	2005	2006	2007	2008
Interest expense					
Total stockholders' equity					
Total short-term loans	-				
Total long-term loans					
Total loans					
Total all other liabilities					
Total liabilities					
Operating income					

Key Ratio Calculations
  1. Times interest earned
Operating income/annual interest expense
  2. Debt to equity ratio
Total liabilities/total stockholders' equity
  3. Long-term debt to equity ratio
Long-term debt/total stockholders' equity					

generate more cash flow and profits. Internal sources of cash may be not only the least expensive source but also the easiest to tap. There are many sources of internal financing, such as the ones that follow.

Reduction of Inventory Levels

Management of inventory is probably one of the most difficult and important jobs within a business. By effectively and efficiently managing inventory levels, cash can be available for other needs. Some of the best ways to reduce inventory levels are contained in Table 12-2.

Profits

When a company makes a profit, whether for a month or year, the owner(s) of a small business can decide to leave the profit in the company or distribute it. By leaving the profit in the business, the equity accounts will increase and help finance the growth of the business or

Table 12-2. Ways to Reduce Inventory Levels (not listed in order of importance)	
1.	Identify and sell slow-moving or obsolete inventory.
2.	Analyze the inventory turnover rate in total and by product line. This should indicate how much time it takes to convert the inventory into cash.
3.	Install or monitor the inventory reorder process to determine reorder points.
4.	Use the ABC inventory method (also called the 80-20 rule) to manage different inventory levels and payments to key vendors.
5.	Determine if some of your key vendors are willing to provide consigned inventory, where the cash is not disbursed for the inventory until it is sold.
6.	If the business has excess inventory, determine what restocking charges (if any) will be incurred if the inventory is returned to the vendors.

fund some of the developing needs. Additionally, the owner may decide to distribute the profit, and may do so through several avenues, such as dividends, increased salary, and bonuses, just to name a few. The owners' actions toward the profits often sends a message regarding what goals they have developed regarding the overall profitability and sustainability of the organization.

Increasing Accounts Receivable Collections

The development and communication of clear policies regarding customer delinquent accounts should take place. If the organization is unclear as to what extent the customer can use credit or the consequence of not paying within the agreed time, it is probably going to have some cash flow problems. Money collected quickly makes the company more profitable. If the business has a sufficient supply of cash on hand, it can take more discounts from its vendors, which translates into operations that are more profitable. Table 12-3 lists some key areas to help collect the accounts receivable faster.

Review Accounts Payable Disbursement Policies

Vendors (accounts payable) can provide a significant source of internal financing. While a primary concern regarding accounts payable may be to maintain or improve the business's overall credit rating, an organization

Table 12-3. Ways to Reduce Accounts Receivable Balances (not listed in order of importance)	
1.	Invoice for the products or services as soon as possible. The sooner the invoice goes out, the sooner the invoice may be scheduled for payment by your customer. In some cases, perhaps the customer can be billed in advance or the billings can be accelerated.
2.	Follow up promptly and consistently on all past-due accounts. When contacting the customer, be firm and ask for a date when the amount will be paid. If the payment is not received within the time period agreed to, again contact the customer on the next date and ask for an explanation and why the amount was not paid. Use whatever facilities are available to expedite the payment process (telephone, e-mail, fax, etc.).
3.	If the organization is not currently accepting major credit cards, explore the possibility of doing so. Make it easy for the customers to be able to pay.
4.	Look at existing incentives for early payment. Perhaps exploring other discount options such as 3/10 net 20, even though it is not part of the industry tradition, may have a significant positive impact on overall cash flow and net profit.
5.	Salespeople who have been assigned specific accounts can be a significant source of assistance in collecting past-due accounts from their customers. When salespeople are calling on specific accounts, make sure they have printouts of who is past due. The salesperson has contact with key personnel at the customers' location, so utilize this to collect the amounts due as well as to make additional sales.
6.	Monitor the status of past-due receivables on a weekly basis, and hold people accountable for collecting the balances.

can do several things to improve its overall cash flow and profitability. Table 12-4 outlines some practical suggestions.

Funding From Shareholders, Family, and Friends

A common way to obtain financing for a small business is from its current shareholders, family, and friends. This may include such things as withdrawing money from a personal savings or investment account, or using personal lines of equity and debt to obtain cash to help the small business. Because the organization is nonpublic, the individuals involved usually have a history of experiences and relationships outside the organization that can be a good source of funding. Depending on the intent for the potential source of cash, the money may be put onto the balance sheet in the form of debt, with a signed promissory note specifying interest and repayment dates, or may be considered equity as shares of stock are issued. Although some consider this infusion of capital as external to the organization, I feel that internal sources provide these funds, meaning relationships to the primary shareholder(s) of the nonpublic company.

Table 12-4. Ways to Effectively Utilize Accounts Payable (not listed in order of importance)	
1.	Take advantage of all discounts. Although each payment term has different cash benefits to the organization, generally it is best to take advantage of the discount. For example, payment terms of 2/10 net 30 translate into an effective interest rate of about 36%. This overall reduction of the cost of products will generally translate into an increase in the overall profit of the organization.
2.	If cash flow problems arise in which specific vendors cannot be paid within the payment terms, take a more proactive approach. Call the vendors and tell them when payment can be expected, thanking them for their patience and understanding.
3.	Pay invoices based on the date the merchandise is received or the invoice date, whichever is later.
4.	For those vendors who offer net discount terms, delay payment until the latest possible date, without affecting the relationship.
5.	Some suppliers may be willing to offer significant volume discounts if an agreement is signed regarding purchasing a specific amount of units or dollar volume over a specified period of time. Explore this opportunity with key vendors.
6.	Some suppliers may offer installment payments, even though the merchandise is shipped in advance. Additionally, other suppliers may offer datings or even merchandise to be shipped on a consignment basis, in which the merchandise is not required to be paid until it is sold.

External Sources of Financing

Once the small business has exhausted the previously discussed internal sources of capital and the controller still needs to find additional resources, external sources may be available. Some of the more popular sources follow.

Lending Institutions

Although commercial banks have been the primary source of funding for many small businesses, other avenues such as credit unions and other cooperative lending organizations are available. Loans from lending institutions may be short-term, such as lines of credit, or may be medium-term loans usually from 3 to 10 years. The interest rates may be fixed or variable, and adjusted periodically based on the loan agreement.

Another source of loans is from overdrafts.[2] Although banks usually charge interest based on the amount overdrawn from period to period, an agreement establishes the limit, and as long as the overdrafts do not exceed the limit, the usual processing of all checks and other forms of payment occurs. Although this method of obtaining financing is an alternative, use with caution as some of the features available through overdrafts may affect the overall banking relationship.

Factoring Accounts Receivable

Another popular source of external financing is the factoring of accounts receivable. Once the receivable occurs, a factor acquires it, usually paying between 75% and 90% for the receivable. When the receivable is collected, payment on the remainder of the receivable occurs, less a fee charged by the factor. This may be a good source of funds for the growing company that needs capital to expand its business. Factoring is not a loan, no repayment is expected, and unexpected effects do not appear on the balance sheet.

Leasing

Although lease agreements have many different structures, the intent of leasing in this context is to be a form of rental, where the lessee makes payments to the lessor under the terms of the lease agreement. Just about any type of asset qualifies for leasing, including vehicles, equipment, and computers. Operating leases may be more appropriate than financing leases for the lessee, if the intent is to utilize the leased item for a relatively short time. Leasing is usually attractive if the lessee does not have enough cash to buy the asset or if the organization would have trouble obtaining financing to buy it. In some cases, leasing can be less expensive than bank loans; however, leasing may be a source for the controller to explore.

Venture Capitalists

These special types of investors usually put money into business and require some form of equity arrangement. Venture capitalists understand the risks associated with investing their money into another company, thus they require a high rate of return. The period for investors is usually 3 to 7 years or more. The initial information required by venture capitalists is extensive, and a high percentage of funding requests are not honored. While some venture capitalists are not usually involved in the day-to-day operations of the business, many are very active in the firm and expect some input into any significant decision made by the organization.

Angel Investors

Another type of investor is the high-net-worth individual who invests money in small firms owned by others. These investors usually invest early in the life of the business and may invest anywhere from $250,000 to $5 million, depending on their understanding of the business and its potential. Similar to venture capitalists, they normally require a high rate of return. Generally, an informal network is necessary to find these sophisticated investors. Angel investors rarely participate in the management of the business; however, their contacts and expertise can be of great value.

Line of Credit and Its Cost

A line of credit is an agreement with a bank to lend up to a specified amount. The company may draw from or pay down the principal amount as it desires, and the company pays interest on the amount actually borrowed, not on the entire balance available.

Depending on the organization's banking relationship, as well as other factors, banks may charge a fee for the availability of the line and, in some cases, may charge a fee for any unused portion of the line. The controller should be cognizant that, in many cases, these fees are negotiable and flexible. The company should ensure it has a committed line of credit, which makes the credit line available even though market or economic conditions may change significantly. This could be important if the business has significant negative changes in its financial performance and position.

Banks usually base their interest charges on a prime rate plus one or more percentage points, as well as the credit worthiness of the business. The prime rate the bank is charging is not the national prime rate, and some room for negotiation is usually available. In addition to an interest rate on the outstanding balance, as well as a fee for the availability of the credit line, it is not uncommon for a bank to require that a certain balance, called a compensating balance, be maintained in its checking account(s) and other accounts within the banking institution. The amount of the credit line outstanding usually reflects these balances. There are many different types of fees for a line of credit, and the controller must know the true effective rate of interest charged by the bank. Table 12-5 shows a sample calculation.

Table 12-5. Calculation of the Effective Interest Cost Based on a Line of Credit

Assumptions:

1. Total line of credit available is $600,000.
2. Interest rate specified in the agreement is 6%.
3. Additional fees charged by the bank: 1% based on the unused portion of the available line of credit and 1% commitment fee to ensure the availability of the line of credit.
4. A 10% compensating balance of the outstanding line of credit is required to be maintained in the checking account.
5. Average outstanding amount on the line of credit is $500,000.

Calculation	
Net amount of cash available for use	
Average outstanding amount on line of credit	$500,000
Less 10% compensating balance required to be maintained in checking account (unavailable for normal use)	**50,000**
Net amount available for use	$450,000
Cost of interest and additional fees	
Interest on borrowed and outstanding line of credit: $500,000 × 6%	$30,000
1% commitment fee on total line of credit available: $600,000 × 1%	6,000
1% based on the unused portion of available line of credit: ($600,000 − $500,000) × 1%	**1,000**
Total cost of interest and additional fees	$37,000
Overall effective interest cost	
$37,000/$450,000	**8.20%**

In this chapter, several techniques have been presented with ideas to help obtain both internal and external sources of cash. We discussed techniques pertaining to inventory, accounts receivable, and accounts payable. We also presented ways to obtain external funding, such as from banks, leasing, venture capitalists, and angel investors. We also presented Tables 12-1 through 12-5, which displayed some of the information. The next chapter discusses taxes for small businesses.

CHAPTER 13

Taxes for Small Businesses

Small businesses need to be aware of the tax implications for business decisions, as well as what sort of taxes, both federal and state, are created by specific types of business entities (sole proprietorship, partnership, S corporation, C corporation, or limited liability company [LLC]). This chapter is not an exhaustive discussion of all types of taxes or a consideration of all the tax implications and ramifications of running a small business; however, several key areas are relevant and important for the small business controller.

This chapter presents various tax issues pertaining to the choice of a business entity. It also discusses changes in fiscal years and differences in net income and taxable income. We explain the differences between book and tax income, along with deferred tax assets, deferred tax liabilities, and permanent and temporary timing differences. We discuss tax administrative matters, along with Form 1099 and other information tax returns. We define the alternative minimum tax (AMT) and suggest ways to take money out of a C or S corporation. We discuss some issues when preparing for an IRS audit, as well as debt versus equity financing by shareholders. Lastly, we present some tax planning strategies, including proper classification of fixed assets, Section 179 deduction, obsolete or unusable inventory, and tax net operating losses.

Choice of Entity

This refers to the legal form of a business. The business form establishes the income tax return(s) filings with the federal government as well as state authorities. The current list of legal forms consists of a traditional C corporation, an S corporation, limited partnerships, general partnerships, limited liability companies, and sole proprietorships. If the incorporated business has filed federal and state tax returns for years, the controller needs to understand some of the intricate aspects of an S versus a C corporation.

A Sole Proprietorship

A sole proprietorship is usually an unincorporated business owned by one person. Being a sole proprietorship determines if the owner will file a Schedule C or Schedule C-EZ and attaches it to his or her individual tax return Form 1040. Schedule C or Schedule C-EZ lists the income and expenses generated during the business year, not to exceed 1 year.

Not only does the sole proprietor pay income tax on its profit or loss listed on the Schedule C or C-EZ, but he or she must pay self-employment tax on the profits. Form SE reports the profit and becomes part of the individual's tax return for the year.

Depending on the amount of business profits and other income or expense items listed on Form 1040, the individual may have to file quarterly estimated tax payments. Form 1040-ES reports the estimated tax payments and is required on a timely basis if at least $1,000 of additional tax is due upon the filing of the tax return. Some exceptions apply as to the payment of estimated tax payments, thus review the current federal tax code for updated information.

Partnerships

A partnership exists when two or more persons engage in a trade or business. The creation of a partnership occurs when each partner contributes money or other business property into the partnership. Partners are not employees of the partnership and should not receive a Form W-2 as employees; however, based on many factors, including such things as the amount of time devoted to the partnership by each partner as well as the specific skills of each partner, the partnership agreement determines the sharing of the profits or losses of the business.

A partnership files an annual information return (Form 1065), which reports its income, deductions (expenses), gains, and losses from its business, but the partnership does not pay federal income taxes. A partnership calculates its income and deductions similar to a sole proprietorship, although some deductions are different for the partnership.

Each partner reports his or her respective share of the partnership profits or losses on their own individual tax return (Form 1040). The partnership is a conduit and uses the pass-through concept to require each individual partner to report his share of the profits or losses.

The partnership provides each partner with a form K-1, which is part of the Form 1065 provided to the Internal Revenue Service (IRS) annually. Based on the K-1 that each partner receives, each individual includes the information on his or her individual Form 1040.

As noted under a sole proprietorship previously, the individual is also required to pay self-employment tax on his or her K-1 and may be required to pay quarterly estimated income tax payments. The $1,000 additional liability noted under sole proprietorship applies also to partners. Check the current federal tax code for some exceptions that may not require the payment of estimated tax payments.

C or S Corporations

When selecting a corporate form of ownership, the shareholders put money and property into the corporation in exchange for shares of ownership within the corporation. A corporation not only has the normal deductions that a sole proprietorship has, but it also has some special deductions to calculate its taxable income.

An S corporation is a regular corporation, much like a C corporation, with shareholders, shares of stock, and bylaws, but its taxation is different. The individual S corporation shareholders report their share of the taxable income or losses from the S corporation and the individual taxpayers realize the "flow-through" tax benefits. There is no double taxation of S corporate income like there is with regular C corporations. However, a C corporation pays tax on profits generated by the corporation, and the individual shareholders receive no tax liability unless distributions occur during the year, creating double taxation. The controller needs to be aware of the requirements for a corporation to become an S corporation, which include a maximum amount of shareholders and each shareholder completing Form 2553 from the IRS.[1] Often, the limited liability company may be a better option than either the S or C corporations; therefore, the controller needs to review the current IRS requirements and seek legal and tax advice before making any changes to the current tax structure.

Limited Liability Company (LLC)

Recently, various state statutes have allowed a new business entity called an LLC. Similar to a corporation, owners of an LLC have no personal liability for the debts or negative actions of management. One important feature is that LLCs are very similar to partnerships in the pass-through taxation discussed previously.

Most states do not restrict ownership within an LLC, and members of an LLC replace shareholders in a corporation. The members (owners) can consist of only one-member (called "single-member") LLCs, corporations, other LLCs, and foreign entities. Additionally, there exists no maximum number of members within the LLC.

Before establishing an LLC, check your individual state requirements and federal tax regulations, as generally, banks and insurance companies cannot be LLCs.

Change in Fiscal Year

Assuming a C corporation has been in existence for a while, the year-end selected, and Form 1120 filed for each fiscal year, it is necessary to obtain prior approval from the IRS before any change occurs in the fiscal reporting period. Form 1128, "Application to Adopt, Change, or Retain a Tax Year" (revised January 2006), accomplishes this request.[2] Generally all corporations requesting a change in its tax year must file Form 1128; however, some exceptions do exist, so the controller should review the IRS's current instructions regarding when and if the form is required to be filed. Part II of Form 1128 contains instructions on when the IRS grants automatic approval. Although the corporation has been in existence for a prolonged period and has had the same fiscal year for tax purposes, it is still possible to change its fiscal year.

Differences in Net Income and Taxable Income

Many companies want the best of both—high net income on its financial statements and low taxable income on its tax return. Generally accepted accounting principles (GAAP) and Internal Revenue Code (IRC) regulations differ, thus causing financial income and taxable income to be different. The amount a business reports as income tax expense is often not the same as income taxes payable to the IRS. The net income generated on a set of financial statements is prepared in accordance with GAAP and intended to provide meaningful and relevant information to its users. However, taxable income complies with the tax code that has a different purpose in mind. The guidance from GAAP and IRS will create differences between book and taxable income. Part of a corporation's tax return is a schedule reconciling differences between net income per books and taxable income per tax return. Differences between income tax expense and income tax payable on a corporation's books creates a deferred tax amount—either deferred tax liability, representing additional taxes owed in the future because of taxable temporary differences, or deferred tax assets, which are taxes saved or refunded because of temporary tax differences during the period. Currently, Financial Accounting Standards Board (FASB) Statement No. 109, "Accounting for Income Taxes," provides guidance on temporary differences and the proper presentation of financial statement amounts.[3] Some of the key terms the controller needs to be familiar with are listed below.

Deferred Tax Assets

Deferred tax assets are on the balance sheet, recognizing temporary differences that result in future deductible amounts (lowering the tax bill). For example, if a corporation recorded in its financial statements a potential loss of $25,000, but the loss would not be deductible for tax purposes until paid, the result would be greater tax deductions in the future creating a deferred tax asset account.

Deferred Tax Liabilities

A deferred tax liability is a balance sheet account used to accumulate amounts that will create future taxable amounts. For example, assume that a corporation accounts for revenue on the accrual basis according to GAAP but records income on its tax return when the cash is received (cash basis), rather than earned. If the sale (in accounts receivable) is uncollected at the end of the year, a deferred tax liability occurs to record the future tax liability pertaining to this transaction, specifically the balance in the accounts receivable account.

Permanent Versus Temporary Timing Differences

Permanent timing differences are items that enter into either taxable income or financial statement income, but not both. For example, the proceeds from life insurance policies carried on key employees or officers of a corporation appear on the income statement of an organization; however, it is not taxable income on the tax return and would be part of the reconciliation from book net income to taxable income. Additionally, permanent differences do not reverse themselves over time, as temporary differences do. The controller needs to ensure the financial statements reflect only temporary timing differences as deferred tax assets or deferred tax liabilities.

Preparation and Filing of 1099s and Other Information Tax Returns

Just about every business needs to file some sort of Form 1099 at the end of each year. Whether the reason is for payment of dividends in closely held businesses, payment of rent on a facility, or payment to outside legal and tax advisors, the IRS requires the filing of appropriate documents. When setting up a new vendor in its accounts payable system, the small business acquires accurate information on Forms W-4, W-9, or both, about the new vendor's taxpayer identification numbers. Backup withholding may be required and reported on Form 945, if the employer does not gather the appropriate forms.[4]

Additionally, backup withholding may also be required if the business has received a notice from the IRS requiring it. Currently, a business can match the taxpayer identification numbers, names, and addresses with the IRS before sending the returns to the IRS by accessing http://www.irs.gov and searching for "e-services."

A multitude of penalties exist when the 1099 is filed, currently ranging from $15 per information return to $50 per return. Additionally, other penalties apply if the correct payee number is not provided, ranging from $50 per return to a maximum of $250,000 per year. Some exceptions to the penalties exist, and Sections 6721 and 6722 contain current information. The 1099s and appropriate accompanying forms are required to be submitted to the IRS by the end of February each year; however, a 30-day extension can be obtained from the IRS. The business sends the recipient's copy of the 1099 by January 31 of each year. The following lists some of the important elements pertaining to 1099 and other filings.

Payments to Corporations and Partnerships

Generally, reporting payments to corporations are not required; however, payments to partnerships usually are required. Some exceptions do exist.

Form 1098

Form 1098 is required for receipt of $600 or more of mortgage interest, including points received in a trade or business.

Form 1099-DIV

Form 1099-DIV is required for payment of $10 or more of dividends and capital gain distributions.

Form 1099-INT

Form 1099-INT is applicable when a trade or business pays $10 or more of interest expense.

Form 1099-MISC

Form 1099-MISC is required for payments of generally $600 or more for rent payments, prizes and awards, services performed for a trade or business who is not an employee, and fees to directors, just to name a few.

Additionally, pension and profit-sharing distributions or any plans in existence during the year providing fringe benefits have reporting requirements.

Alternative Minimum Tax (AMT)

Some corporations may be subject to an AMT, which arises because some tax laws give special treatment to different types of income and expenses. The purpose of the AMT is to ensure that all corporations pay a minimum amount of tax on its reported profits.[6] A corporation would owe AMT when its minimum tax reported on its corporation tax return is more than its regular tax. A corporation defined by the IRS as a small corporation is not subject to the AMT and pays no minimum tax. Generally, the requirements for a small corporation are that prior to 1997, the IRS classified the business as a small corporation, and its annual gross receipts for the last 3 tax years did not exceed $7.5 million. Generally, the corporation files Form 4626[7] with the corporation's annual tax return if its adjustments and preferences, as defined by the IRS, exceed $40,000. This is an important area for controllers to be aware of if they are responsible for the tax planning aspect of the business.

Taking Money Out of S and C Corporations

Taking money out of an S corporation is much easier than taking it out of a C corporation. Owners of an S corporation can take money out of the corporation whenever they desire without any tax implications by receiving a distribution of profits. However, when organized as a C corporation, the amounts distributed to the shareholders, called dividends, are double-taxed—once to the corporation since they are paid out in after-tax dollars, and once to the individual receiving the distribution. In both a C and S corporation, shareholders can receive additional funds by salary payments, as well as interest on loans made to the corporation. Make sure the shareholders receive reimbursement for all expenses incurred as this is a tax deduction for the corporation but is not taxable income to the employee or shareholder.

Preparing for an IRS Audit

Based on recent statistics, the IRS audits approximately only 2% of small business tax returns.[8] The best way to prepare for an IRS audit is to make sure as the year is progressing that all properly recorded transactions and sufficient documentation is available before the IRS requests it. Ensure that the small business maintains corporate records and retained for a specified period, in accordance with company policy and IRS guidelines. The IRS conducts about one-third of tax audits performed via the mail where they ask the taxpayer to verify or explain specific items.[9] The IRS may want to audit a specific item on the tax return or may ask for an explanation on how a certain amount pertains to the trade or business. A consultation with an outside tax advisor may occur before responding to the IRS, depending on the circumstances. However, be sure to respond to the IRS in a timely and professional manner, addressing fully the questions asked. If the controller does not wish to appear before the IRS (if so requested), he or she can sign a power of attorney on behalf of the corporation, allowing an accountant, lawyer, or enrolled agent admitted to practice before the IRS to represent the corporation at the IRS audit.

The corporation also has other rights, and the controller may want to review the IRS Web site before proceeding with the audit requirements. Additionally, certain appeal rights exist that may be pursued.

Debt Versus Equity Financing by Shareholders

When a shareholder or employee has decided to put additional resources (cash or other things of value) into a nonpublic company, generally it is better for both the corporation and the shareholder to put the money into the corporation in the form of debt versus additional equity. The loan should be in writing specifying an interest rate and repayment dates. Additionally, the transaction should appear in a corporate resolution indicating a need for the funds and authorizing the corporation to enter into the transaction with the shareholder. A prime reason for putting funds into the corporation as debt rather than equity is that interest payments are tax deductible by the corporation whereas dividend distributions are not. Additionally, the shareholder has the ability to get the debt out of the corporation tax free because the payments are not distribution of profits. This eliminates the double taxation issue described previously. The controller may want to consult an outside accounting firm for other advantages and disadvantages before putting the money into the corporation.

Tax Planning Strategies

Effective techniques to reduce corporate taxes can be an important part of a controller's responsibilities. Before action occurs, the controller should develop a strategy and schedule to outline the overall taxes saved with possible implementation of new ideas and techniques. Below are some items the controller may want to consider when planning an overall tax strategy.

Proper Classification of Fixed Assets

Based on several criteria, the IRS categorizes an item for depreciation purposes. For example, if computer equipment (which is classified by the IRS as 5-year property) is mistakenly classified as office furniture and equipment (which is 7-year property), depreciation deductions will be allocated over 7 years versus the correct period of 5 years.

Make Use of the Section 179 Deduction

Section 179 of the Internal Revenue Code[10] allows corporations to expense fully tangible personal property (not real estate) in the same year purchased. Based on the current tax code for 2008, a business can expense and immediately deduct $250,000 in capital expenditures. There are some other limitations so the rules and regulations for Section 179 should be reviewed; however, based on the 2009 code, the maximum annual acquisition of deductible property is $800,000. After obtaining the $800,000, the overall deduction reduces dollar for dollar. The overall deduction for Section 179 may also be limited to the amount of taxable income. The type of property that qualified for the

Section 179 treatment is machinery and equipment, some computer software, and furniture and fixtures.

Obsolete or Unusable Inventory

Review the inventory periodically to see if some slow-moving items are obsolete or unusable. If so, take them out of inventory and either discard or donate them to a charitable organization. Inventory not saleable or in good condition should not be valued, in compliance with GAAP and IRS guidelines.

Tax Net Operating Losses

If a corporation has a net operating loss for the current year, it has the option of carrying back the losses 2 years and forward 20 years or electing to carry forward the losses for 20 years. The exercise of the carry forward option occurs in the year of the loss. Otherwise, the company carries back the loss. The controller should be aware of IRS Form 4466,[11] which if filed, requires the IRS to act on it within 45 days of receipt. When carrying back the loss to obtain a refund of the previous year's income taxes paid, the filing of Form 1139[12] occurs and requires the IRS to act within approximately 90 days as compared to the traditional time of 3 to 6 months when filing an amended return.

Reporting Employee Fringe Benefits

A business has reporting requirements for the various employee fringe benefits provided. The IRS defines a fringe benefit as a form of pay for the employee working. The small business controller should have an appreciation for the many items to consider when ensuring the business compliance with IRS reporting regulations. The controller should review Publication 15-B from the IRS, which states that all fringe benefits are taxable unless specifically excluded by law.[13]

Tax Administrative Matters

A controller may be the individual responsible for fully discharging tax administration matters. A tax calendar that outlines important due dates for complying with federal and state tax requirements is recommended. For example, the controller needs to know the filing requirements and due dates for tax forms. Additionally, they need to know when estimated state and federal tax payments are required, know when payroll tax returns and tax payments for both the employees and the employer's payroll taxes are due, and keep track of what is required on a daily basis and when completed. In some cases, the controller may not have the proper experience and training and must seek outside professional help.

In this chapter, taxes for small businesses were discussed. The choice of entity and the corresponding tax impact of each entity were discussed. We presented topics including differences between net income and taxable income, including a discussion of deferred tax assets and liabilities. We introduced Form 1099, as well as several current tax planning strategies for the small business.

Chapter 14 introduces the small business controller to internal controls and the development of an effective internal control structure.

CHAPTER 14

Internal Controls

This chapter addresses the responsibility of the small business controller regarding internal controls. It also defines internal controls; the value of internal controls; developing an internal control structure considering such factors as the control environment, risk assessment, control activities, information and communication, and monitoring and feedback; key elements to consider when designing a good internal accounting control structure; limitations of internal controls, and the overall responsibility for internal controls.

The Controller and Internal Controls

Perhaps one of the most important duties of the controller for a small business is the creation, supervision, and maintenance of financial accounting internal controls. These responsibilities might involve such things as reviewing the existing control structure, making whatever changes are necessary, and implementing, if necessary, new internal controls. To assess effectively internal controls, the controller should have knowledge of different types of fraud that may develop within an organization and some ways to help deter it. To gain this knowledge, a controller may need to perform a complete assessment of the procedures pertaining to all functions within the activities of the organization, concentrating on the controls relevant to the proper recording of accounting transactions. For example, the controller needs to ascertain that proper checks and balances are in place, that the available personnel are competent and trustworthy, that a review of the authorization procedures occurs on a periodic basis to ensure compliance, and that a proper segregation of duties and responsibilities is happening to reduce the probability of errors.

Definition of Internal Controls

An integral part of any organization's financial policies and practices is its internal controls. The definition of internal controls is many; however, for the purpose of this book, this author uses the Committee of Sponsoring Organizations (COSO) definition: "Internal control is a process to provide reasonable assurance of accomplishing objectives. Specifically, it helps achieve objectives relating to the reliability of financial reporting, compliance with laws and regulations, and effectiveness and efficiency of operations."[1]

All organizations, whether public or nonpublic, profit or nonprofit, large or small, need to have an understanding of how the internal control structure should work as compared to how it is working. The quality of financial and nonfinancial information presented depends on an adequate system of internal controls. Although Section 404 of the far-reaching Sarbanes-Oxley Act of 2002 (SOX) does not specifically apply to small businesses, many privately held companies are adopting some of its requirements as best practices.

The Value of Internal Controls

Stakeholders other than shareholders, including bankers, major vendors, officers, and the board of directors, just to name a few, realize how important internal controls are to an organization, especially small businesses. For example, in some cases, if a small business is seeking director or officer liability insurance, a review of internal controls and other criteria by an insurance company may affect the premiums.

A key element in the internal control process is deterring fraudulent activities. Although strong internal controls provide no guarantee of preventing fraudulent behavior, controls that are effective and closely monitored help to produce accurate and reliable financial information.

Developing an Internal Control Structure

According to COSO's definition of internal control, the effectiveness of an internal control system can be measured by assessing five components:

the control environment, risk assessment, control activities, information and communication, and monitoring.[2]

The first factor, the control environment, according to COSO, consists of the tone at the top, where the organization's administration and leaders in each department assess such factors as ethical values, leadership philosophy, and policies and procedures.[3]

Risk assessment is the second factor, and every organization has various risks from internal and external sources. Risk assessment is the process of identifying and analyzing potential risks and deciding how to manage those risks.[4] Control activities usually consist of establishing policies and procedures. Although top management may have established control activities, the activities must permeate throughout the entire organization, affecting such important aspects as segregation of duties and responsibilities for employees.[5]

The fourth element of internal control is information and communication. People from all levels within the organization must interact and communicate on a regular basis, as most activities affect other activities. This communication must take place up and down, as well as across, different levels of the entire organization.[6]

The last item within this five-component matrix is monitoring and feedback. The internal controls evolve over time and require evaluation on a regular basis. Just as the assessment of risks changes, the way various job functions are performed also changes with technology and changes in personnel, and an update of the internal controls is necessary to keep abreast of these changes.[7]

Limitations of Internal Controls

The cost-benefit rule as it pertains to internal controls specifies that the costs of implementing and monitoring a specific control should not exceed its expected benefits. Even though the installation and monitoring of internal controls may require a significant amount of time, energy, and money, some factors may cause the system to be ineffective. For example, turnover of employees as well as new employees finding innovative and creative ways to perform the necessary tasks to get the job done may override the controls initially set up, and a revision may be necessary. No system is perfect, and the human ability to override a system is sometimes more powerful than the system itself. Realize that any system has limitations and can be overridden, circumvented, or altered without the person responsible for the control knowing that it is happening. Internal control in the workplace requires a system of checks and balances.

If the controller of a small business is utilizing the services of an outside Certified Public Accounting firm, they often ask for a checklist of specific areas and questions to ask during the planning and continuous monitoring stages of the internal control system. The controller needs to select the requirements of internal control that applies to their organization.

Overall Responsibility for Internal Controls

Although the controller of a small business may take the leadership role in designing and altering internal control policies and procedures, they are not the only one responsible for internal controls. The Foreign Corrupt Practices Act of 1977, although pertaining primarily to publicly held companies, requires multinational corporations to be aware of its internal control systems. Controllers of nonpublic companies and small businesses should be aware of the requirements of the act and realize it became law because of allegedly domestic political contributions and bribery of foreign government officials.

In this chapter, we discussed internal controls within a small business and the controller's role. We defined internal controls and the development of an internal control structure. We also discussed the overall responsibility for internal controls and their limitations.

The next chapter discusses the changing role of the small business controller and ethical considerations.

CHAPTER 15

The Changing Role
of the Controller

The role of the controller in a small business has changed dramatically over the past number of years. Today's controller often performs many tasks that were not part of a controller's role a few years ago. For example, today the small business controller may be responsible for not only the internal audit function but also the information technology function. As the business environment has changed, new and different skills are required for the controller to master these tasks efficiently and professionally.

Depending on the size of the organization and its structure, even the title of the controller may change. Some common names for controllers are controllers, comptrollers, office managers, treasurers, and one of the newest titles is chief accounting officer. Although chief accounting officer is perhaps the most appropriate title, in this book I refer to the position as controller, regardless of how an organization defines the role. Whatever the title, the controller is an integral part of the management team that directs the financial affairs of an organization in most small businesses.

Joining Professional and Trade Associations

Controllers need to become knowledgeable about problems facing the industry in which they work. Trade associations can provide valuable support in this area, as well as provide excellent reference material and personal contacts.

Joining various accounting associations, such as local chapters of the Institute of Management Accountants (IMA) and the State Society of Certified Public Accountants, provides valuable networking resources. Getting involved in the local Chamber of Commerce and other professional groups will provide good networking opportunities and give the controller some recognition for his relationship within the community and the type of products and services that his company provides. Some of the networking contacts could prove to be very valuable in the future, especially if the controller is seeking a new banking relationship or looking for a new insurance agent or broker, for example.

However, although it is necessary for the controller to get out of the office environment and become part of the professional and business community, he must be careful not to take on too much too quickly. He should not volunteer to serve on committees or become an officer of these organizations until he understands how much time will be required to fulfill his controllership responsibilities. He should not overextend himself before he is acclimated to the new management position and continuing family responsibilities.

Controllers need to decide which, if any, professional or trade associations are of interest to them. Some controllers choose to spend some time working with charitable organizations, while others choose to get involved with trade or professional groups. Whatever the area of interest, controllers need to be involved in community activities on some level.

Ethics and Ethical Challenges

A controller of a small business often encounters challenging ethical issues. These issues may arise due to such things as, among others, decreasing cash flows, lack of profits, and pressures from business competitors. The controller may confront illegal or fraudulent activities. If the controller is a Certified Public Accountant (CPA), a Certified Management Accountant (CMA), or a Certified Fraud Examiner (CFE), he could lose his license if convicted of criminal acts or ethical violations.

Need for Code of Ethics

In many cases, the controller provides the ethical guidance and preparation of a code of ethics for a small business. This code of ethics should consider all levels of the organization, including the board of directors and officers. Many Web sites are available to offer guidance on how to prepare a written code of ethics for an organization, and additionally, the controller may be able to obtain a copy of other similar companies' codes of ethics by asking members of management of the organization, as well as contacting various trade and professional associations. However, merely having a code of ethics is not enough. All levels within the organization must adhere to the code by example, not merely by words.

The code of ethics will vary from company to company, depending on many factors including size. However, a number of elements should be part of a common code. Some of these elements address such issues as receiving or giving gratuities and gifts, confidential information, and conflicts of interest. As noted previously, it is not enough to have a code of ethics. It is important that all new employees review the code and sign a document that they will comply with the code. On a continuing basis, all employees should be required annually to sign a document stating that they understand the company's code of ethics and that they have and will comply. In addition, employees should be aware of the process to report unethical behavior.

Depending on what professional associations the controller belongs to, such as the American Institute of Certified Public Accountants (AICPA), the Institute of Management Accountants, or the Association of Certified Fraud Examiners (ACFE), just to name a few, each organization has its own code of ethics or, in some cases, a professional code of conduct addressing such things as maintaining confidentiality as it pertains to sensitive financial information, a high level of competence, a high level of personal integrity, and objectivity. For example, the AICPA has principles of professional conduct that address serving the public interest, objectivity and independence, and due care.[1] The IMA has a statement of ethical professional practice, which contains the elements of competence, confidentiality, integrity, and credibility,[2] while the ACFE provides a code of professional standards and includes professional conduct in the areas of integrity and objectivity, professional competence, due professional care, and confidentiality.[3] These codes are quite specific, and some offer a toll-free telephone number for those seeking confidential advice. Additionally, each professional accounting association has its own standards of ethics, which should help to guide the practicing controller. In many cases, the controller can also receive help from other professional accounting associations.

When controllers face ethical issues, whether it is to make an inappropriate adjustment to financial statements, to sign an incorrect tax return, or to delay depositing federal, state, or other payroll taxes withheld from employees, they need to understand the process within the company's organizational structure to resolve the issue. The controller should contact their next immediate supervisor who is not involved in the unethical situation. If that does not resolve the issue, the next level, which could be the owner, president, or CEO of the company, needs to be contacted by the controller. When all internal means are exhausted and the problem is still unresolved, the controller should seek personal legal counsel. In some cases, the controller may have to resign. Unless the controller is legally required to do so, he should not disclose the issues to any regulatory authority or anyone outside the company. If the controller does resign, he should write a memo to the owner or CEO of the company outlining the facts and the reasons for the resignation.[4]

In this last chapter, we discussed the changing role of the controller, joining professional and trade associations, ethics and ethical challenges, and the need for a small business code of ethics. Lastly, we discussed several professional accounting associations' codes of ethics as examples.

We hope you have enjoyed this book, and welcome any comments to r.hanson@snhu.edu.

Notes

Chapter 1

1. *Small business* (2009).

Chapter 3

1. *Session 1: Users and suppliers of financial statement information* (2009).
2. *Accounting department management report* (2005).
3. *Accounting department management report* (2004).

Chapter 4

1. American Institute of Certified Public Accountants (AICPA) (2008a). Effective for financial statements submitted after December 31, 2000.
2. AICPA (2008a). Effective for financial statements submitted after December 31, 2000.
3. AICPA (2008b). Effective for audits beginning on or after December 15, 2002, unless otherwise indicated.
4. AICPA (2008c). Effective for reports issued or reissued on or after January 1, 1989, unless otherwise indicated.

Chapter 5

1. *B-cash cycle* (2006).
2. *What idle cash?* (2005).

Chapter 6

1. *Regulation B. Appendix C—sample notification forms* (2006).
2. *Security interests—the basics* (2006).
3. Abrams (2008).
4. *Business owner's toolkit. Accounting for bad debts* (2006).
5. IRS (2006).

Chapter 7

1. Schreibfeder (2005).

2. *Carrying cost of inventory* (2005).

3. *Determining the reorder point: How low should I let my inventory level go before I reorder?* (2005).

4. Kieso, Weygandt, and Warfield (2005)

5. SMC Data Systems (2005).

6. Schreibfeder (2006).

7. Schreibfeder (2006).

Chapter 8

1. Loring & Company (2009).

2. *Exemption certificate* (n.d.).

3. *Security agreements* (2009).

4. TechDuke (2009).

Chapter 9

1. *Financial analysis revised. Session 2: Project evaluation and selection analysis techniques* (2006).

2. *Table 3: Present value factors and time value of money* (2006).

Chapter 10

1 *Cost of capital* (2006).

2. McClure (2003).

3. *Debt to equity ratio (financial leverage ratio)* (2006).

4. Simkins (2006).

5. RMA (2006).

Chapter 11

1. *Free cash flow—FCF* (2009).

2. Financial Accounting Standards Board (1976).

3. IRS (2009h).

Chapter 12

1. *Sources of finance* (2009).
2. *How to stop overdrawing a checking account* (2009).

Chapter 13

1. IRS (2009d).
2. IRS (2009b).
3. Financial Accounting Standards Board (1992).
4. IRS (2009g).
5. *Section 6721 failure to file correct information returns* (2009).
6. IRS (2009f).
7. IRS (2009f).
8. *How to avoid an IRS audit* (2009).
9. *How to avoid an IRS audit* (2009).
10. *The section 179 deduction* (2009).
11. IRS (2009e).
12. IRS (2009c).
13. IRS (2009a).

Chapter 14

1. Hubbard (2003).
2. Hubbard (2003).
3. Hubbard (2003).
4. Hubbard (2003).
5. Hubbard (2003).
6. Hubbard (2003).
7. Hubbard (2003).

Chapter 15

1. *AICPA code of professional conduct* (2009).
2. *IMA statement of ethical professional practice* (2009).
3. *ACFE CFE rules and regulations* (2009).
4. *IMA statement of ethical professional practice. Resolution of ethical conflict* (2009).

References

Abrams, S. (2006). *P-card programs—An all-inclusive tool for the global supply chain*. Retrieved March 5, 2008, from http://www.mastercard.com/us/company/en/docs/ePayments.pdf

Accounting department management report. (2004, June). Retrieved March 5, 2009, from http://www.ioma.com

Accounting department management report. (2005, February). (Issue 05–02). Retrieved March 5, 2009, from http://www.ioma.com

ACFE CFE rules and regulations. (2009). Retrieved March 3, 2009, from http://www.acfe.com/about/cfe-rules.asp?copy=ethics

AICPA code of professional conduct. (2009). Retrieved March 3, 2009, from http://www.aicpa.org/About/code/index.html

American Institute of Certified Public Accountants (AICPA). (2008a, July 16). AR Section 100 Compilation and Review of Financial Statements.

American Institute of Certified Public Accountants (AICPA). (2008b, July 16). AU Section 316 Consideration of Fraud in a Financial Statement Audit (SAS No. 99 and Statement on Auditing Standard No. 113).

American Institute of Certified Public Accountants (AICPA). (2008c, July 16). AU Section 508 Reports on Audited Financial Statements.

B-cash cycle. (2006). Retrieved March 8, 2006, from http://www.peio.net/Courses/finanal/ch/ch8b.html

Business owner's toolkit. Accounting for bad debts. (2006). Retrieved November 3, 2006, from http://www.toolkit.cch.com/text/p02-5651.asp

Carrying cost of inventory. (2005). Retrieved November 3, 2005, from http://www.investopedia.com/terms/c/carryingcostofinventory.asp

Cost of capital. (2006). Retrieved February 15, 2006, from http://en.wikipedia.org/wiki/Cost_of_capital

Debt to equity ratio (financial leverage ratio). (2006). Retrieved February 15, 2006, from http://www.bizwiz.ca/debt_equity_ratio.html

Debt vs. equity? (2005). Retrieved October 29, 2005, from http://www.dynamicequity.com/vcmag03.htm

Determining the reorder point: How low should I let my inventory level go before I reorder? (2005). Retrieved November 3, 2005, from http://office.microsoft.com/enus/assistance/HA01126021033.aspx

Exemption certificate. (n.d.). Retrieved from West Virginia Department of Revenue. West Virginia Consumers Sales and Service Tax and Use Tax—Form WV/CST-280 (Rev. 905).

Financial Accounting Standards Board. (1976, November). *Statement of financial accounting standards no. 13. Accounting for leases.* Norwalk, CT: FASB.

Financial Accounting Standards Board. (1992, February). *Statement of financial accounting standards No. 109 accounting for income taxes.*

Financial analysis revised. Session 2: Project evaluation and selection analysis techniques. (2006). Retrieved December 11, 2006, from http://cbdd.wsu.edu/kewlcontent/cdoutput/TR505r/page15.htm

Free cash flow—FCF. (2009). Retrieved April 22, 2009, from http://www.investopedia.com/terms/f/freecashflow.asp

How to avoid an IRS audit. (2009). Retrieved April 23, 2009, from http://www.wwwebtax.com/audits//audit_avoiding.htm

How to stop overdrawing a checking account. (2009). Retrieved April 22, 2009, from http://www.ehow.com/how_2122566_stop-overdrawing-checking-account.html

Hubbard, L. D. (October 2003). Internal auditor. *Understanding internal controls: Auditors who can accurately interpret COSO's internal control framework offer great value to management.* Retrieved March 4, 2009, from http://findarticles.com/p/articles/mi_m4153/is_5_60/ai_110222002

IMA statement of ethical professional practice. (2009). Retrieved March 3, 2009, from http://www.imanet.org/about_ethics_statement.asp

IMA statement of ethical professional practice. Resolution of ethical conflict. (2009). Retrieved March 4, 2009, from http://www.imanet.org/about_ethics_statement.asp

IRS. (2006). *Topic 453—bad debt deduction.* Retrieved March 24, 2006, from http://www.irs.gov/taxtopics/tc453.html

IRS. (2009a). *Employer's tax guide to fringe benefits* (Publication 15-B). Retrieved April 6, 2009, from http://www.irs.gov/publications/p15b/ar02.html

IRS. (2009b). *Instructions for form 1128 request for a change in fiscal year.* Retrieved April 10, 2009, from http://www.irs.gov/instructions/i1128ch01.html

IRS. (2009c). *Instructions for form 1139 net operating loss carry back for small businesses.* Retrieved April 5, 2009, from http://www.irs.gov/newsroom/article/0,,id=205329,00.html

IRS. (2009d). *Instructions for form 2553 election by a small business controller.* Retrieved April 10, 2009, from http://www.irs.gov

IRS. (2009e). *Instructions for form 4466 corporation application for quick refund of overpayment of estimated tax.* Retrieved April 6, 2009, from http://www.irs.gov

IRS. (2009f). *Instructions for form 4626 alternative minimum tax – corporations.* Retrieved April 6, 2009, from http://www.irs.gov/taxtopics/tc556.html

IRS. (2009g). *Instructions for form 945 annual return of withheld federal income tax.* Retrieved April 6, 2009, from http://www.irs.gov

IRS. (2009h). *Internal Revenue Service—United States Department of the Treasury.* Retrieved April 22, 2009, from http://www.irs.gov/publications/p535/ch03 .html

Kieso, D. E, Weygandt, J. J., & Warfield, T. D. (2005). *Intermediate accounting* (11th ed.). Chapters 8 and 9. Hoboken, NY: John Wiley & Sons.

Loring & Company. (2009). *Insurance company audit procedures.* Retrieved March 5, 2009, from http://www.loringco.com/insurance_company_audit _procedures.asp

McClure, B. (2003). *Investors need a good WACC.* Retrieved February 10, 2006, from http://www.investopedia.com/printable.asp?a=articles/fundamental/03/ 061103.asp

Regulation B. Appendix C—sample notification forms. (2006). Retrieved October 25, 2006, from http://www.bankersonline.com/regs/202/202-appc.html

RMA. (2006). *Robert Morris Associates changes its name to RMA—The Risk Management Association.* Retrieved February 11, 2006, from http://www.rmahq .org

Schreibfeder, J. (2005a). *EIM the mysterious cost of carrying costs.* Retrieved November 3, 2005, from http://www.effectiveinventory.com/article35.html

Schreibfeder, J. (2006). *EIM cycle counting can eliminate your annual physical inventory! (part one).* Retrieved April 14, 2006, from http://www.effectiveinventory .com/article9.html

The section 179 deduction. (2009). Retrieved April 6, 2009, from http://www .section179.org/section_179_deduction.html

Section 6721 failure to file correct information returns. (2009). Retrieved April 6, 2009, from http://caselaw.1p.findlaw.com/casecode/uscodes/26/subtitles/f/ chapters/68/subchapters/

Security agreements. (2009). Retrieved March 5, 2009, from http://www .smartagreements.com/product_preview.php

Security interests—the basics. (2006). Retrieved October 25, 2006, from http:// debtor-creditor.lawyers.com/creditors-rights/Security-Interests----The-Basics.html

Session 1: Users and suppliers of financial statement information. Retrieved March 30, 2009, from http://cbdd.wsu.edu/kewlcontent/cdoutput/tr505r/page43 .htm

Simkins, B. (2006). *Case studies in corporate finance. Cost of capital teaching notes.* Retrieved February 15, 2006, from http://mysearch.myway.com/jsp/ GGmain.jsp?searchfor=hurdle+rates&st=dwd&ptnrS

Small business. (2009). Retrieved March 3, 2009, from http://www.en.wikipedia
.org/wiki/Small-business

SMC Data Systems. (2005). *Just in time inventory control systems from SMC Data
Systems.* Retrieved November 3, 2005, from http://www.smcdata.com/just-in
-time-inventory-controlsystems-1.html

Sources of finance. (2009). Retrieved April 22, 2009, from http://www.bized
.co.uk/learn/accounting/financial/sources/index.htm

Table 3: Present value factors and time value of money. (2006). Retrieved May 4, 2006,
from http://72.14.207.104/search?q=cache:12Bn7rfHCaEJ.www.studyfinance
.com/common

TechDuke. (2009). *Beware of restocking fees—return policies.* Retrieved March 5,
2009, from http://www.techduke.com/2007/06/12/beware-of-restocking-fees
-return-policies/

What idle cash? (2005). Retrieved November 3, 2005, from http://www.agribusiness
-mgmt.wsu.edu/ExtensionNewsletters/cash-asset/idleCash.pdf

Index

Note: The italicized *t* and *f* following page numbers refer to tables and figures.